THE DISMISSAL OF STUDENTS WITH MENTAL DISORDERS:

☐ *Legal Issues*

☐ *Policy Considerations and*

☐ *Alternative Responses*

By GARY PAVELA, J.D.

The Higher Education Administration Series
Edited by Donald D. Gehring and D. Parker Young

COLLEGE ADMINISTRATION PUBLICATIONS, INC.

College Administration Publications, Inc.,
P. O. Box 8492, Asheville, N. C. 28814

Library of Congress Cataloging in Publication Data
Pavela, Gary, 1946-
    The dismissal of students with mental disorders.

    Bibliography: p.
    Includes index.
1. College students—Legal status, laws, etc—
United States. 2. School expulsion—Law and legislation
—United States. 3. Mental health laws—United
States. I. Gehring, Donald D. II. Title.
KF4243.P38 1985   344.73'07914   85-13227
ISBN 0-912557-01-X   347.3047914

This monograph is adapted from an article by the
author, "Therapeutic Paternalism and the Misuse of
Mandatory Psychiatric Withdrawals on Campus" 9
Journal of College and University Law 101 (1982-83).
Published jointly by the National Association of Col-
lege and University Attorneys and the West Virginia
University College of Law.

The views expressed in this book are those of the
author and are not necessarily those of College
Administration Publications, Inc.

This publication is designed to provide accurate and
authoritative information in regard to the subject
matter covered. It is sold with the understanding that
the publisher is not engaged in rendering legal, ac-
counting or other professional service. If legal advice
or other expert assistance is required, the services of
a competent professional person should be sought.
*—from a Declaration of Principles jointly adopted by a
committee of the American Bar Association and a committee of publishers.*

Table of Contents

Appendix II
Case Studies • 71

Foreword

This monograph, the second in the Higher Education Administration Series, was written in response to what we as the series editors see as a growing area of concern. There have always been students with serious mental disorders attending our postsecondary institutions. The line between genius and a mental disorder may be very thin. In recent years, however, there seems to be a heightened awareness of the problems generated on campus in dealing with students who have some form of mental disorder.

As editors of *The College Student and the Courts* we have seen an increase in the number of cases reported that involve students with alleged mental disorders. Anyone reading their local newspaper or the professional literature cannot help but be aware of the increased problem of suicides, attempted suicides, depression, and various eating disorders which exist on our campuses. Other forms of neuroses and psychoses can also be observed—some that are manifested in violent behavior.

Very few college and university administrative or counseling practitioners, however, have received any formal professional training in dealing with such students from a legal and a policy perspective. Some institutions respond to the problem by invoking a mandatory withdrawal policy. Others deal with the problem from a strictly disciplinary approach and some, never having had a problem in the past, refuse to face the issue.

Developing a policy that defines institutional responses to students with serious mental disorders is imperative. The purpose of this monograph is to assist in constructing such a policy. The author discusses, in a very readable style, the legal parameters within which your policy should be developed. But the monograph is not simply a legalistic approach to the problem. The author presents a well reasoned humanistic perspective that integrates constitutional, statutory and case law with ethical and counseling considerations.

Those who already have a policy may also find the monograph helpful. The legal and policy considerations presented in the monograph may be used as standards against which current institutional policies may be measured. The case studies offer excellent staff training materials.

Not only will the monograph be of value to administrators who have broad policy responsibilities, but psychiatrists, psychologists and counselors will also find the publication helpful. The monograph outlines many of the legal responsibilities of these practitioners and it provides a basis for the discussion of ethical considerations with administrative colleagues. Those who have direct dealings with campus judicial processes (i.e., attorneys, judicial affairs officers and housing administrators) will also find the monograph to be an invaluable resource and a vehicle for developing different perspectives on the issues. Graduate faculty who teach legal issues courses will be delighted with the wealth of discussion material contained in the publication. The blend of law and ethical considerations make the monograph a perfect supplemental text for graduate courses.

There is no substitute for legal counsel. This monograph is intended only as a beginning point to generate discussion on campus and to point out broad legal and policy considerations. Counsel can be extremely helpful in reviewing institutional policy after thorough discussion of the educational aspects has taken place.

Donald D. Gehring
D. Parker Young
Series Editors
June, 1985

About the Author

Gary Pavela, J.D., is Director of Judicial Programs at the University of Maryland–College Park, where he also teaches courses in constitutional and administrative law. He is a member of the New York bar, has been a law clerk to a judge of the United States Court of Appeals for the Tenth Circuit, a fellow at the University of Wisconsin Center for Behavioral Science and Law, and a consultant to the Federal Judicial Center in Washington, D.C.

Mr. Pavela is a Phi Beta Kappa graduate of Lawrence College in Wisconsin, holds advanced degrees in history and in education from Wesleyan University in Connecticut, and a law degree from the University of Illinois. He has extensive experience in higher education administration, including positions in residence life, student services, academic affairs, and university legal counsel. His articles have appeared in the *Journal of College and University Law*, *The School Law Journal*, and *The Chronicle of Higher Education*, among others.

Chapter I

Introduction

In 1976, the President of the University of Michigan distributed a memorandum on his campus pertaining to "Incidents Involving Individuals Who Appear to Have a Mental, Emotional, or Behavioral Disorder Which Impels Them to Actions Threatening the Safety of Others." He reported that "[t]here have been a few incidents during the fall term involving individuals who appear to have some mental, emotional or behavioral disorder. . . . In one case, an individual apparently set eighteen fires in various campus buildings before being apprehended." The President concluded that university disciplinary procedures "were not drawn with this type of problem in mind" and he established an ad hoc procedure to bar certain students from campus "until such time as we are given reasonable assurances that present psychiatric problems have been successfully resolved" (Fleming, 1976).

The policy developed at the University of Michigan is not unique. A recent survey of 123 institutions of higher education revealed that the majority of them have found it necessary to make some provision for the mandatory "medical" or psychiatric withdrawal of students (Steele, Rickard, Johnson, 1984, p. 340). Several of those schools removed more students on psychiatric grounds than were expelled for disciplinary reasons. Furthermore, comparable withdrawal policies are being routinely applied to students who threaten or attempt to commit suicide (Bernard and Bernard, 1980).

One common characteristic of most mandatory withdrawal policies is ambiguous language. Students may be withdrawn at some campuses because their "state of mind" so "recommends,"* or because they are suffering a "disturbance," or simply because they "cannot

---

*Examples cited throughout the text are drawn from materials supplied to me by twenty-five diverse institutions of higher education from across the country.

benefit from the available services of [university] therapeutic agencies." One institution has a policy of withdrawing students "in those cases where counseling and evaluation require it to be the proper action." The withdrawn student is then sent the following standardized letter:

> [w]e regret that the effect of your present health condition upon you as a person and upon the college community requires that you receive immediate medical attention during which time you will be placed on medical leave of absence. You are hereby withdrawn . . . This action is supported by the professional judgment of appropriate college officials and is in your best interest at this time.

These policies have been developed as alternatives to the traditional disciplinary process on some campuses, or as a means to remove mentally ill students who are unable to meet academic requirements, or to remove students who threaten or attempt to commit suicide. However well intended, many of the policies reflect insufficient attention to a number of important legal issues and policy considerations, including the scope of Section 504 of the federal Rehabilitation Act of 1973 (29 *U.S.C.* 794, 1976); the substantive and procedural constitutional standards which would be applicable at public institutions; the accuracy of psychiatric diagnoses; and the role of the campus disciplinary process. This monograph addresses each of these issues, and contains sample standards and procedures for mandatory withdrawals. In addition, a number of case studies and suggested responses have been provided for use in college or university staff training exercises.

Chapter II

The Impact of Section 504 of the Rehabilitation Act of 1973 on Mandatory Withdrawal Policies

One of the more significant laws affecting the mandatory withdrawal of students with mental disorders is the Rehabilitation Act of 1973. This Act and its implementing regulations mandate specific actions to be taken by educational institutions concerning students or applicants with handicaps. The part of the Act specifically related to colleges and universities is known as Section 504, which provides, in part:

[n]o otherwise qualified handicapped individual . . . shall, solely by reason of his handicap, be excluded from the participation in, be denied the benefits of, or be subjected to discrimination under any program or activity receiving Federal financial assistance . . . (29 *U.S.C.* 794, 1982).

A "handicapped" individual is defined as "any person who (i) has a physical or mental impairment which substantially limits one or more of such person's major life activities, (ii) has a record of such an impairment, or (iii) is regarded as having such an impairment" (29 *U.S.C.* 706 (7) (B), 1982). Major life activities mean "functions such as caring for one's self, performing manual tasks, walking, seeing, hearing, speaking, breathing, learning, and working" (45 *C.F.R.* 84.3 (j) (2) (ii), 1980). The words "physical or mental impairment" have been defined in the regulations to include "any mental or psychological disorder" such as "emotional or mental illness" (45 *C.F.R.* 84.3 (j) (2) (i) (B), 1983).

With respect to post-secondary and vocational education, the regulations define a "qualified" handicapped person as an individual "who meets the academic and technical standards requisite to admission or participation in the recipient's education program or activity," (45 *C.F.R.* 84.3 (k) (3), 1983). The regulations then state that:

[n]o qualified handicapped student shall, on the basis of handicap, be excluded from participation in, be denied the benefits of, or other-

wise be subjected to discrimination under any program or activity which receives or benefits from Federal financial assistance. (45 C.F.R. 84.4 (a), 1983).

Relevant portions of Section 504 and related regulations have generally been interpreted to the benefit of recipient institutions. It is useful, however, to review several of those interpretations in order to consider the precise ways in which the Act may affect mandatory withdrawal policies comparable to those cited in the introduction.

WHAT SECTION 504 DOES NOT PROHIBIT

The inclusion of "mental and psychological disorders" within the coverage of the Act has not been construed to mean that a recipient college or university must ignore or excuse the behavioral manifestations resulting from such disorders. In 1977, before final interpretative regulations were issued, the United States Attorney General released a formal opinion pertaining to Section 504 which affirmed that "[a] person's behavioral manifestations of a disability may . . . be such that his . . . participation would be unduly disruptive to others, and Section 504 presumably would not require unrealistic accommodations in such a situation" (43 *Op. Atty. Gen.* No. 12, 1977, p. 2). A similar conclusion was reached by the Department of Health, Education and Welfare (now Department of Health and Human Services), which advised in an "Analysis of Regulation" that a recipient may hold a drug addict or alcoholic (or, presumably, any person suffering from a comparable mental impairment) "to the same standard of performance and behavior to which it holds others, even if any unsatisfactory performance or behavior is related to" the person's mental impairment (45 *C.F.R.* 84, 1983, App. A. at 298; see also, 1978 Amendments pertaining to current users of alcohol or drugs, 29 *U.S.C.* 706 (7) (B) (Supp. 4, 1980)). In short, according to the HEW analysis, the statute and regulations were designed to prohibit the exclusion of a handicapped student at a recipient institution of higher education only "if the person can successfully participate in the education program and complies with the rules of the college and if his or her behavior does not impede the performance of other students" (45 *C.F.R.* 84, 1983, App. A at 299).

A further restriction of the potential coverage of Section 504 resulted from the Supreme Court's 1979 decision in *Southeastern Community College*, (1979). Holding that the refusal of an educational institution to admit an individual with a serious hearing impairment did not constitute a violation of Section 504, the Court rejected the argument that the Act required recipient educational institutions "to make substantial modifications in their programs to allow disabled persons to participate." Essentially, it was held that a "qualified handicapped individual," as defined by the statute, "is one who is able to meet all of a program's requirements *in spite of* his handicap." (Emphasis sup-

4

plied). Although the Court did suggest that "situations may arise where a refusal to modify an existing program" to accommodate a handicapped person "might become unreasonable and discriminatory," that suggestion was made in the context of the Court's reference to possible "technological advances" and would not appear to require a recipient institution of higher education to modify "reasonable rules of conduct" in order to accommodate a person suffering from a mental disorder (*Southeastern Community College*, 1979, p. 405-413).

The reasoning in *Southeastern Community College* was recently applied and amplified by the United States Court of Appeals for the Second Circuit in a case specifically involving a mental disorder. In *Doe* (1981b), the Court of Appeals reversed the grant of a preliminary injunction requiring the medical school at New York University to readmit a former student who claimed she had been denied readmission solely because of her previous history of psychiatric difficulties. The *Doe* case, of course, requires considerable development here, in light of the nature of Doe's handicap and because of the analysis offered by the Court of Appeals.

Jane Doe (a pseudonym) gained admission to the medical school at New York University in 1975 after falsely representing on her application that she had not had any chronic "emotional problems." In fact, Doe had previously suffered from a series of psychiatric problems, including self-destructive behavior, and had been committed to a mental hospital. Doe's previous history was subsequently discovered after her enrollment, but New York University allowed her to continue her studies with the understanding that she would be expected to withdraw from school if her psychiatric problems recurred. Shortly thereafter, in January 1976, Doe engaged in self-destructive behavior (bleeding herself with a catheter so she "could cope with her stress") and she agreed to withdraw, with the understanding that she might request reinstatement (*Doe*, 1981b, p. 767). Doe was hospitalized shortly after her withdrawal and was diagnosed as having a serious mental disorder requiring extensive treatment over a number of years.

Doe reapplied to the New York University Medical School in June of 1977, contending that she had received psychiatric treatment and that she had "ceased altogether her self-destructive behavior and learned alternate, healthy forms of behavior to deal with stressful situations" (*Doe*, 1981c, Brief of Appellee, p. 5). New York University ultimately denied Doe's application, after arranging for her to be interviewed by a New York University psychiatrist and after reviewing favorable letters of evaluation from two psychiatrists who had treated her. Doe then filed a lawsuit in the United States District Court for the Southern District of New York, asking the court to compel her readmission "on the ground that she was an otherwise qualified handicapped person whom New York University had excluded . . . solely on the basis of her history of mental impairment in violation of

Section 504" (*Doe*, 1981c, Brief of Appellee, p. 7). While awaiting the outcome of what became a very protracted lawsuit, Doe obtained a Masters Degree in Health Policy and Management at Harvard University and was successfully employed as a program analyst with the Department of Health, Education and Welfare. She received several favorable letters of evaluation from her supervisors, including a former Surgeon General of the United States, who found her "extremely conscientious and very highly respected by her colleagues" in a "very demanding" work environment (*Doe*, 1981c, Brief of Appellee, p. 10).

In 1981, approximately five years after Doe withdrew from New York University, the District Court granted a preliminary injunction requiring New York University to readmit her. It was held that Doe was "handicapped" within the meaning of Section 504, that she had established that she was "otherwise qualified," in spite of her handicap, and that New York University had not met its burden of showing "that the plaintiff was not otherwise qualified, or that the rejection . . . was for reasons other than handicap" (*Doe*, 1981a, p. 23-24). The court concluded that New York University's reasons for rejecting Doe were based upon "unfounded factual conclusions" (*Doe*, 1981a, p. 24) and observed that:

> [a]lthough this court could (and ultimately may have to) listen to all of the earnestly offered psychiatric diagnosis . . . the court finds the plaintiff's actual behavior and condition over the past five years to be more reliable criteria for predicting her future behavior [and that] she will more likely than not be able to complete her course of medical studies and serve creditably as a physician. (p. 14)

New York University immediately appealed the district court decision, which was speedily reversed by the Second Circuit Court of Appeals in an opinion which all but decided the case before it ever went to trial. Essentially, it was held that although Doe should be classified as a handicapped person under Section 504, she had failed to show "that despite her handicap she is qualified" for admission to the New York University Medical School. The "crucial question" was "the substantiality of the risk that [Doe's] mental disturbances will recur, resulting in behavior harmful to herself and others." The court held that there was a "significant risk" of such recurrence and, even if the risk was simply "appreciable," that factor "could properly be taken into account in deciding whether among qualified applicants, it rendered [Doe] less qualified than others for the limited number of spaces available." The court also observed that although Section 504 "requires us rather than the institution to make the final determination of whether a handicapped individual is 'otherwise qualified' . . . considerable judicial deference must be paid to the evaluation made by the institution itself . . ." (*Doe*, 1981b, p. 776-779).

The holding by the Court of Appeals in *Doe* may be limited by the fact that Doe was found to have a "serious" mental disorder likely to "continue through most of . . . her adult life" (*Doe*, 1981b, p. 768). Also, the case may not be fully applicable to undergraduate education, since the court concluded that there were "exceptional stresses" associated with medical training (*Doe*, 1981, p. 788). A person suffering from a mental disorder similar to Doe's might be capable of meeting institutional requirements in other academic programs, including graduate education (*Doe*, 1981b, p. 788). Nonetheless, the case does reinforce an interpretation of Section 504 which would allow a recipient institution to take into account the likely recurrence of harmful behavior by a person suffering from a mental disorder. Accordingly, *Doe*, along with *Southeastern Community College*, the HEW analysis and the cited 1977 Attorney General's opinion, demonstrate that Section 504, by itself, would not necessarily preclude the psychiatric withdrawal or exclusion of students from institutions of higher education. Furthermore, it is clear, at least in the Second Circuit, that the courts will accord considerable deference to relevant evaluations or determinations made by college and university officials.

WHAT SECTION 504 DOES PROHIBIT

Having some idea of what Section 504 apparently does not preclude may offer an insight into what is precluded, and why a poorly drafted psychiatric withdrawal policy could be applied in a way which would run afoul of the Act. Essentially, every relevant interpretation of Section 504 has distinguished between a simple diagnosis of a mental disorder and the behavior resulting from such a disorder. The latter, if it indicates that the student cannot meet reasonable institutional standards, might be sufficient grounds for exclusion. It would not be sufficient, however, to exclude a student:

1. simply because the student was suffering from a mental disorder, or had a mental disorder in the past;
2. because it was assumed, without sufficient supporting evidence, that a student would be unable to meet reasonable institutional standards simply because the student was suffering from a particular mental disorder;
3. because, out of paternalistic concern, it was hoped that a student suffering from a mental disorder (who nonetheless, continued to meet reasonable academic or conduct standards) would obtain treatment elsewhere.

These conclusions are supported by language in the *Doe* case itself. The court of appeals warned that institutional regulations which "serve no other purpose than to deny an education to handicapped persons" would be invalid. Likewise, the court observed that "care must be exercised by schools . . . not to permit prior mental illness to be routinely regarded as a disqualification" (*Doe*, 1981b, p. 779). Furthermore, in a case not involving medical education, the same federal appellate court held that a New York City Board of Education plan to isolate children carrying serum hepatitis virus violated Section 504, since the Board had been "unable to demonstrate that the health hazard posed by the . . . children was anything more than a remote possibility." The Court observed that "while Section 504 has been the subject of infrequent litigation thus far, this Court and others confronting adverse action based on a physical handicap have implicitly assumed that the government agency or other federal funds recipient must establish in court a justification for its action" (*New York State Ass'n for Retarded Children*, 1979, p. 644-49).

It is not necessary to rely entirely upon a process of elimination in order to speculate about the likely impact of Section 504 on psychiatric withdrawals from institutions of higher education. The recent holding by the United States Court of Appeals for the Tenth Circuit in *Pushkin* (1981) offers more substantive guidance, albeit in a different context.

In *Pushkin*, the Court of Appeals affirmed a lower court determination that a rejected applicant to a psychiatric residency program had been discriminated against solely by reason of his handicap (multiple sclerosis and presumed "emotional instability" resulting therefrom) (*Pushkin*, 1981, p. 1382). Pushkin, a medical doctor confined to a wheelchair, had applied to a University of Colorado psychiatric residency program and was interviewed by four faculty members of the University of Colorado Psychiatric Hospital. The mean ratings from Pushkin's interview were held to be too low for admission, resulting in his rejection and his subsequent lawsuit.

A critical finding by the trial court in *Pushkin*, supported by the Court of Appeals, was that the observations of the interviewing panel were "not predicated on any known deficiency of Dr. Pushkin himself," but were based upon the interviewers' "general knowledge" of multiple sclerosis "and their concern for psychologic reactions [of patients] and in turn the doctor, as a result of his being in a wheelchair" (*Pushkin*, 1981, p. 1386). Individual interviewers, as quoted or paraphrased by the court, concluded, for example, that Pushkin had "a lot of anger" which he was "unaware of or cannot deal with;" that he was "teachable," but would be unable "to face the [reactions] that can be stirred up in his patients by his physical condition;" that he was unable, as a result of his handicap, to withstand "the emotional stress of treating patients;" that he "had emotional problems" and "was emotionally upset"; and that his work "would make him unhappy" (*Pushkin*, 1981, p. 1389).

Pushkin's interviewers, however, had met with him for only 45 minutes before forming their conclusions, and were contradicted at the trial by another University of Colorado psychiatrist, who treated Pushkin and had observed him for four years. The latter, who also interviewed potential medical residents at Colorado (not including

Pushkin), was "apprehensive about testifying in opposition to his employers," but affirmed that Pushkin was "well within the norm of emotional control and behavior;" that he "treated . . . patients appropriately" and "reasonably well understood their feelings toward him;" and that Pushkin was a "responsible, reasonable, reasoned and conscientious physician" (*Pushkin*, 1981, p. 1389).

The Court of Appeals in *Pushkin* endorsed the trial court's conclusion that the interviewers' reasons for rejecting Pushkin were based upon "incorrect assumptions or inadequate factual grounds" (*Pushkin*, 1981, p. 1383) and that those reasons had been effectively rebutted. The University's argument that Pushkin was, in any event, less qualified than other applicants was also rejected, since it was "not supported by the record" and had not been articulated in the original interviewers' reports (*Pushkin*, 1981, p. 1382). Also, the court observed that the University's actions highlighted the fact that "[d]iscrimination on the basis of handicap . . . often occurs under the guise of extending a helping hand" and may be based upon "a mistaken, restrictive belief as to the limitations of handicapped persons" (*Pushkin*, 1981, p. 1385). Above all, what seemed of particular concern to the Court of Appeals was the fact that the "conclusions of the examining board rest on psychologic theory. Our reaction is that these are weak and inadequate threads where, as here, the entire future of the plaintiff is at stake" (*Pushkin*, 1981, p. 1391).

The Tenth Circuit's reasoning in *Pushkin* appears to be distinctly different from that followed by the Second Circuit in *Doe*. That difference, however, may be more illusory than real. Given the facts as found by the trial court in *Pushkin*, the result reached there is entirely consistent with the warning in *Doe* that schools should not "routinely" regard a handicap as a disqualification. In the context of mandatory psychiatric withdrawals, therefore, both cases support the conclusion, as set forth above, that recipient institutions of higher education should conduct a careful inquiry into whether a student suffering from a mental disorder has engaged in some demonstrable behavior which indicates that he or she can "reasonably" be viewed as posing a "substantial risk" of being unable to meet "reasonable [institutional] standards" (*Doe*, 1981, p. 775). If this analysis is correct, the literal application of psychiatric withdrawal policies permitting students to be summarily removed simply "for reasons of mental health" or because students "cannot benefit from . . . [university] therapeutic agencies" will remain a potential source of liability under Section 504.

SUMMARY
Section 504 of the Rehabilitation Act of 1973 does prohibit discrimination against individuals suffering from a mental disorder.

However, the Act and related regulations have not been construed to mean that a recipient college or university must excuse the behavioral manifestations resulting from such disorders. A properly drafted code of student conduct or withdrawal policy may be relied upon to remove students who pose a danger to themselves or to others, or who directly and substantially impede the lawful activities of others on campus.

Chapter III

Constitutional Issues Affecting Mandatory Withdrawal Policies

In addition to a possible violation of the federal handicap regulations, there are a number of other legal issues which might arise in the context of any decision to remove a student from campus on psychiatric grounds. Perhaps the most important, at public institutions, would be whether or not the student's constitutional rights had been violated.

Many educators have criticized the overbroad, vague, confusing, and occasionally preposterous standards for student conduct which used to be encountered at campuses across the country. Two well known examples are the dismissal of a student who was "apparently not in sympathy with the management of the institution" (*Woods*, 1924, p. 550) and the expulsion of a Syracuse University student for not being "a typical Syracuse girl" (*Anthony*, 1928, p. 438). Most schools began to discard such standards in the 1960s, perhaps as a result of litigation (see, e.g. *Soglin*, 1968), or in response to urgings from various national educational organizations (see the "Joint Statement on Rights and Freedoms of Students," 1967). The operative principle, of course, was that students should not be subject to arbitrary dismissals based upon regulations which failed to state with sufficient precision what was or was not acceptable behavior.

Although disciplinary rules are being written with greater specificity, some campuses have chosen to adopt mandatory withdrawal policies which could serve as unintended parodies of student conduct regulations at the turn of the century. Now, instead of being expelled for "conduct prejudicial to the school" (*Dixon*, 1961, p. 150) students are "withdrawn" because their "state of mind" so "recommends"* or

---

*The cited example is from a mandatory withdrawal policy developed at a public university on the East Coast.

11

because their mental health renders them "undesirable" (*Aronson*, 1981, p. 781). Indeed, the similarity between the old disciplinary standards and the new "medical" ones is so striking that one suspects that the latter were appropriated in their entirety from college catalogues of the 1950's (or earlier) and dressed up with suitable therapeutic nomenclature. The end result, of course, is the same, or worse: students are stigmatized and dismissed on the basis of unintelligible standards which are readily subject to arbitrary and discriminatory application.

FREEDOM OF EXPRESSION AS AN ISSUE
IN MANDATORY WITHDRAWAL POLICIES

The most dangerous misapplication of any broadly worded mandatory withdrawal policy would be to dismiss socially or politically "eccentric" students who had not engaged in any behavior which posed a danger to themselves or others, or which substantially disrupted normal university activities. It was precisely this danger, (in the context of overbroad disciplinary regulations) which most concerned Professor Charles Alan Wright, who wrote in a 1969 *Vanderbilt Law Review* article that "[i]f the institution is no longer free to discipline a student because he peacefully expresses unpopular political views, how easy it would be to proceed against him indirectly on the ground that an unkempt appearance or bizarre clothes violated the interdictions about 'good taste' and 'proper conduct'" (Wright, 1969, p. 1064-65).

Generally, at public institutions, the courts have been unwilling to tolerate the type of abuse feared by Professor Wright. Recently, for example, in *Shamloo*, (1980), the U.S. Court of Appeals for the Fifth Circuit declared that a university regulation which authorized only "wholesome" demonstrations was unconstitutionally vague. The court observed that a school regulation "is unconstitutionally vague if people of common intelligence must guess at its meaning and differ as to its application" and that "[t]he regulation must not be designed so that different officials could attach different meanings to the words in an arbitrary and discriminatory manner" (p. 523-24).

The holding in *Shamloo* follows a long line of cases indicating that courts will require public educational institutions to give "scrupulous protection" to the First Amendment rights of students, (*West Virginia*, 1943, p. 637). Perhaps the best known of those cases, *Tinker* (1968), held that some forms of behavior (e.g., wearing an armband) can be "the type of symbolic act that is within the free speech clause of the First Amendment" (p. 505). Such symbolic acts cannot be prohibited on the basis of "undifferentiated fear or apprehension of disturbance" (p. 508). Instead:

[i]n order for the State in the person of school officials to justify prohibition of a particular expression of opinion, it must be able to show that its action was caused by something more than a mere desire to avoid the discomfort and unpleasantness that always ac-

company an unpopular viewpoint. Certainly where there is no finding and no showing that engaging in the forbidden conduct would 'materially and substantially interfere with the requirements of appropriate discipline in the operation of the school,' the prohibition cannot be sustained (p. 509).

It certainly is true that most psychological or psychiatric withdrawal policies are not designed to restrict freedom of expression on campus. Nonetheless, an overbroad policy could be used to accomplish that result, since it is all too easy to associate a mental disorder with the expression of unpopular social and political views (see, e.g., *In re Sealy*, 1969). For example, Ennis and Litwack cite a study which indicates that:

> mental health professionals view patients who express radical political views as more disturbed than patients who voice the same psychiatric complaints, but whose political views are more conventional. [The study also found] that voicing criticism of the mental health profession . . . may substantially increase a patient's psychopathology in the eyes of mental health professionals, while flattering the profession tends to decrease a patient's symptomatology (Ennis and Litwack, 1974, p. 728).

This perspective should not come as a surprise. The best confirmation of the potential for such political bias was the willingness of nearly 2,000 psychiatrists to engage in "diagnosis by mail" of Barry Goldwater for *Fact* Magazine in 1964 (Barton, 1968).

Basically, by relying on a broadly written psychological or psychiatric withdrawal policy, school officials could readily remove deviants in order to assure their "needs" would be met by "therapy" elsewhere, and that their activities would no longer disturb or "cause concern" to other students. Indeed, at those institutions where conventionality is valued more than intellectual ferment, the malleable standards found in most psychiatric withdrawal policies could be used to withdraw (and to stigmatize as "mentally ill") the most thoughtful, sensitive, intelligent, challenging and socially committed students at the school.

It is doubtful that most courts, having prevented direct assaults against civil liberties in public schools in the 1960's and 1970's, would now permit educators to circumvent those holdings through the facile use of "therapeutic" language. The Supreme Court has rejected similar efforts by state officials in the past, (see *In re Gault*, 1967) and reiterated in *Healy* (1972) that First Amendment rights "are protected not only against heavy handed frontal attack, but also from being stifled by more subtle governmental interference" (p. 183). In the specific context of psychiatric evaluation and treatment, Chief Justice Burger has observed that "[w]here claims that the State is acting in the best interests of an individual are said to justify reduced procedural and substantive safeguards, this Court's decisions require that they be 'candidly appraised'" (*O'Connor*, 1975, p. 586). The Supreme Court reaffirmed this perspective in *Addington* (1979) when it held that the deprivation of a constitutionally protected "liberty" interest calls for a showing that an individual said to be mentally ill "suffers from something more serious than is demonstrated by idiosyncratic behavior" or "a few isolated instances of unusual conduct" (p. 427).

First Amendment Summary

A legal challenge to the psychiatric withdrawal of a student at a public institution, based on the right to freedom of expression, would focus upon issues not unlike those which might be raised in litigation based upon an alleged violation of Section 504 of the Rehabilitation Act of 1973. The fundamental focus of inquiry would be on whether a student purportedly suffering from a mental disorder has engaged in behavior which indicates that he or she poses a threat to self or others, or is unable to meet other reasonable institutional requirements. The removal of a student based upon vague and unintelligible standards, or simply because the student was a harmless eccentric, or expressed unpopular views, or on the basis of any other calculated pretext, would raise serious First Amendment issues, and probably would not withstand careful judicial scrutiny.

DUE PROCESS CONSIDERATIONS

A common characteristic of many mandatory psychological or psychiatric withdrawal policies is the almost complete absence of procedural safeguards for students subject to withdrawal (Bernard and Bernard, 1980, p. 112). Generally, students will simply be withdrawn by a school psychologist or psychiatrist, or by a student affairs administrator acting upon a recommendation from a mental health professional. The student may be unable to challenge the evaluation which resulted in his or her removal (including any underlying factual accounts or assumptions which influenced it), or to submit an independent psychiatric assessment, or even be informed of the precise nature of the "diagnosis" in question. These policies may be forbidden by a broadly worded requirement for institutional "grievance procedures," set forth in regulations implementing Section 504 of the Rehabilitation Act of 1973 (45 *C.F.R.* 84.7 [b]). However, even in the absence of Section 504 regulations, public schools* are precluded by the Four-

---

*Private schools are probably not required by the Fourteenth Amendment to accord due process protections to students. See, generally, Kaplin, *The Law of Higher Education* (1978) at p. 26 ("to date private postsecondary institutions have won many more state action cases than they have lost"). For an argument that constitutional standards should be applied to private schools, see Schubert, "State Action and the Private University" 24 *Rutgers Law Rev.* 323 (1970). Courts may, however, impose comparable procedural requirements based upon contract theory. Furthermore, private schools may wish to develop significant procedural safeguards as a means of establishing that a mandatory withdrawal was based upon a finding that the student posed a "substantial risk" of being unable to meet "reasonable institutional standards." New York University was successful in the *Doe* case largely for this reason.

teenth Amendment from depriving students of protected "liberty" or "property" interests without due process of law. It is probable that a psychological or psychiatric withdrawal implemented pursuant to a policy offering little or no procedural protection, would be held to constitute a deprivation of liberty or property in violation of the Fourteenth Amendment.

Originally, the framers of the Fourteenth Amendment were concerned about the rights of black people in the Southern courts after the civil war. As a result, the due process clause was designed to insure that persons would not be deprived of their life, their personal liberty, or their property as a penalty for a crime, without a fair trial (Berger, 1977, p. 201). Over the years, however, the terms "liberty" and "property" have been broadly defined by the courts to include a "liberty interest" in one's good name and reputation (*Wisconsin*, 1971) or a "property interest" in certain benefits provided by the state, such as free public education for elementary or high school students (*Goss*, 1975). Furthermore, the "due process" requirement has been applied to state proceedings other than criminal trials, including college and university disciplinary cases (*Dixon*, 1961).

Before determining that a public institution has violated the Fourteenth Amendment, it is necessary to define what precise liberty or property interest has been infringed. The pertinent Supreme Court decisions, however, are often conflicting or ambiguous, indicating that the Court remains divided on this issue. Essentially, in the context of psychological or psychiatric withdrawals from public institutions of higher education, it is possible that either a liberty or property interest may be implicated, although the deprivation of "liberty" (by the imposition of a stigma associated with a finding of mental or emotional "illness") is most likely to invoke some due process protection.

The Mental Illness Stigma
as a Deprivation of Liberty

In *Wisconsin* (1971) the Supreme Court held that "[w]here a person's good name, reputation, honor, or integrity is at stake because of what the government is doing to him, notice and an opportunity to be heard are essential" (p. 437). Shortly thereafter, in *Board of Regents* (1972), the Court reaffirmed *Wisconsin* and observed that "[i]n a Constitution for a free people, there can be no doubt that the meaning of 'liberty' must be broad indeed" (p. 572). Although the Court rejected the respondent's contention that the state's failure to reemploy him in a teaching position constituted a deprivation of liberty, it did note that "in declining to rehire the respondent, [the state] did not make any charge against him that might seriously damage his standing and associations in his community . . . [h]ad it done so, this would be a different case" (p. 573).

The basic formula in *Wisconsin* and *Board of Regents* was readily applied in a number of relevant lower court cases. For example, in *Greenhill* (1975) the United States Court of Appeals for the Eighth Circuit held that when the academic dismissal of a medical student was accompanied by notice to a medical school association that the student "lack[ed] intellectual ability," the student was entitled to an informal hearing with the administrative body dismissing him (p. 7). In *Wellner* (1973), the same court required the institution to give a hearing to a faculty member who was not reappointed, since the presence in the faculty member's employment file of charges that he was a racist "deprived [him] of an interest in liberty which entitled him to a prior hearing, despite his nontenured status" (p. 156).

Likewise, in *Lombard* (1974), the United States Court of Appeals for the Second Circuit held that a probationary teacher had a right to a "full hearing" prior to being discharged as "unfit for duty" due to a report which suggested that he had a mental disorder. Using language which would be especially pertinent in the case of a mandatory withdrawal of a student from a public institution of higher education, the court observed that "[a] charge of mental illness, purportedly supported by a finding of an administrative body, is a heavy burden for a young person to carry through life. A serious constitutional question arises if he has had no opportunity to meet the charge by confrontation in an adversary proceeding." In this case the plaintiff was:

> deprived of his reputation as a person who was presumably free from mental disorder. Without his being given the right to confront witnesses, the termination of his probationary employment was recommended by the Committee of the Superintendent on the primary ground: 'illogical and disoriented conversation, causing request for examination by the Medical Department, which found him unfit for duty.' This is not only a finding but a stigma. If it is unsupportable in fact, it does grievous harm to appellant's chances for further employment, as indeed the record demonstrates, and not only in the teaching field. For that reason he was entitled to a full hearing (pp. 637-638).

Must the Stigma be Made Public?

Holdings such as those in *Greenhill, Wellner* and *Lombard* would be more compelling were they not subject to challenge on the ground that the Supreme Court has now refined its earlier definition of a constitutionally protected liberty interest. Probably the most significant of the Court's refinements, as set forth in *Bishop* (1976), was that an employee discharged for serious misconduct would not be deprived of liberty unless the reasons for the employee's discharge were made public. A literal application of this reasoning, of course, would mean that the liberty interests of a state university student dismissed without a hearing on psychiatric or any other grounds would not be

16

infringed so long as the reasons for dismissal remained confidential. Given the constraints of the Family Educational Rights and Privacy Act on release of student education records (34 *C.F.R.* 99.30, 1981), and assuming the absence of a protected property right, a literal application of *Bishop* would have the potential to undo all of the procedural protections at state colleges and universities mandated by courts since the 1960s.

It is not at all clear, however, that *Bishop* will be literally applied to dismissals of students from public institutions, since dismissal from a college or university may be "inherently" more stigmatizing than termination of employment. Employment termination may affect future job prospects elsewhere, but it would not, in itself, limit educational opportunities as well. On the other hand, removal from campus (or even interruption of attendance) may substantially affect both employment *and* educational opportunities, and preclude certain career choices altogether. Perhaps the best example of the latter consequence can be found in *Glassman* (1970). There, in upholding the denial of admission to a prospective medical student with a history of mental illness, the court cited the policy of the admissions committee to consider prior "interruptions in an academic career" as a negative factor (p. 4).

Also, *Bishop* may not be fully applicable in the educational setting because students would have no choice but to release their confidential records if they wished to obtain educational opportunities elsewhere. The Supreme Court appeared to recognize this issue in *Goss* (1975) (decided just one year before *Bishop*), when it held that the suspension of a number of secondary school students without notice and some kind of a hearing violated the students' protected property and liberty interests. In defining the dimensions of the applicable liberty interest, the Court did not require any immediate public disclosure of harmful information. Instead, it was sufficient that charges of misconduct were simply "recorded." Such recorded charges would not only "seriously damage the students' standing with their fellow pupils and their teachers" but could also "interfere with later opportunities for higher education and employment" (p. 575).

It may also be significant that the Supreme Court had an early opportunity to apply *Bishop* in the context of a student dismissal from a public university, but declined to do so. Instead, in *Board of Curators* (1978) the Justices engaged in extensive "arguments and counterarguments . . . as to the extent or type of procedural protection" required (p. 109) before a medical student at a state university could be dismissed for academic deficiencies, even though the school had not publicized any reasons for the dismissal. There simply was no logical reason for arguments of that nature to have occurred if a majority of the Court regarded *Bishop* as being dispositive of the case, especially since

Horowitz, the student in *Board of Curators*, had not asserted that she had been deprived of a property interest.

The Special Nature of the Mental Illness Stigma

The Supreme Court's holding in *Goss*, and its unwillingness to apply the *Bishop* rationale in *Board of Curators*, suggest that certain stigmas imposed by the state without due process might infringe a protected liberty interest, regardless of publication. Three recent Supreme Court decisions, *Parham* (1979), *Addington* (1979) and *Vitek* (1980) support this conclusion in the specific context of psychiatric labeling.

In *Parham*, the Court defined minimum due process requirements to be followed when parents or guardians seek admission of their minor children to state mental institutions. Chief Justice Burger, writing for the majority, concluded that a formalized proceeding with a neutral factfinder was unnecessary, partly because such a proceeding would pose a danger of a "significant intrusion into the parent-child relationship" (p. 610). On the issue of a child's liberty interest in good name and reputation, the Chief Justice distinguished "diagnosis and treatment" from "labeling." The former, when part of a voluntary commitment procedure, may be less stigmatizing than the public reaction to one who exhibits the symptoms of mental illness (pp. 600-601). Significantly, however, Chief Justice Burger also suggested that psychiatric labeling may be equated with the stigma of a criminal conviction if the individual is labeled by the state as being "mentally ill and possibly dangerous" (p. 600). In any event, for purposes of the decision, it was to be "assumed" that "a child has a protectable interest not only in being free of unnecessary bodily restraints but also in not being labeled erroneously by some because of an improper decision by a state official" (p. 601).

Chief Justice Burger also wrote the majority decision in *Addington* (1979), and used even more expansive language to define the relevant liberty interests of adults subject to involuntary commitment proceedings. Essentially, it was determined that the "clear and convincing" standard of proof was required in such proceedings, partly because a lower standard would not reflect a proper recognition of the "indisputable" fact that:

> involuntary commitment to a mental hospital after a finding of possible dangerousness to self or others can engender adverse social consequences to the individual. Whether we label this phenomena 'stigma' or choose to call it something else is less important than that we recognize that it can occur and that it can have a very significant impact on the individual (pp. 425-426).

The cited quotation in *Addington* was turned against the Chief Justice in *Vitek* (1980), when the Court (with Chief Justice Burger dissenting) held that the involuntary transfer of a state prisoner to a mental hospital required a full "adversary hearing" (p. 495). The issue in the case, of course, was not the deprivation of physical liberty, since that had been accomplished pursuant to a criminal conviction. Instead, the Court was especially concerned about the "stigmatizing consequences" resulting from a finding that the prisoner was suffering from a mental illness. Such a finding required significant procedural safeguards, not only because the individual might be subject to "unwelcome treatment," but because of the prisoner's interest "in not being arbitrarily classified as mentally ill. . . ." (p. 495).

Altogether, the holdings in *Parham*, *Addington*, and *Vitek*, do not contain any suggestion that a finding of mental illness, made without sufficient procedural due process, would have to be publicized by the state in order to constitute a deprivation of a liberty interest in one's good name or reputation. Perhaps the Court simply assumed, as in the case of public school dismissals in *Goss* (1975), that such a finding would inevitably be made public at a later time (see Justice Stewart's concurring opinion in *Parham*, p. 622). It is also possible that the Court may consider psychiatric labeling by the state to be so intrinsically damaging and dehumanizing as to require at least minimal due process protection, especially if the individual suffers the deprivation of some additional, tangible interest. Whatever the reason, the narrow definition of liberty set forth in *Bishop* has not been fully and literally applied by the Court in a number of cases which could be readily analogized to the summary psychiatric withdrawal of a student from a public institution of higher education.

It is, of course, extremely difficult and hazardous to predict how the Supreme Court will define a protected liberty interest in any specific case. Nonetheless, there is no apparent reason why a college student dismissed on psychiatric grounds from a public school has any less interest in "not being arbitrarily classified as mentally ill" than the incarcerated felon in *Vitek*. The most prudent course, at public institutions, would be to follow the guidance offered by the Second Circuit in *Lombard*, and to assume that the courts will continue to regard the mental illness stigma as a sufficiently "heavy burden for a young person to carry through life" to require at least some procedural protection.

How Much Procedure is Due?

The determination that a student subject to a mandatory withdrawal is entitled to some due process protection does not resolve the question of the amount of procedural due process which will be required. The basic factors involved in making that decision are set forth in *Mathews* (1976):

first, the private interest that will be affected by the official action; second, the risk of an erroneous deprivation of such interest through the procedures used, and the probable value, if any, of additional or substitute procedural safeguards; and finally, the Government's

19

interest, including the function involved and the fiscal and administrative burdens that the additional or substitute procedural requirement would entail [Citations omitted] (p. 335).

In applying the *Mathews* criteria, it is reasonable to conclude that a student has a significant interest in avoiding the interruption of an academic career and the imposition of a stigma associated with a finding of mental illness. The latter is a particularly severe consequence which can affect an individual for a lifetime (Rosenhan, 1973, p. 254; Stensrud and Stensrud, 1980, p. 495). The use of various euphemisms (i.e., withdrawing a student on "medical" grounds) or describing inappropriate behavior without using the words "mental disorder," are no guarantee of protection, as can be seen in the *Lombard* case (p. 16, supra). There, the effort to dismiss a public employee on the ground that his "illogical and disoriented conversation" required "examination by the Medical Department" which found him "unfit for duty" was readily perceived by the Court of Appeals as a "charge of mental illness" (pp. 637-638). Such a charge entitled the employee to significant due process protections.

The hazards of psychiatric labeling are compounded by the fact that the risk of error inherent in psychiatric diagnosis is concededly great (see Ennis and Litwack, 1974). As a result, the courts might be inclined to require a number of important procedural safeguards, such as the right to counsel and an opportunity to cross examine the mental health professional making the diagnosis (see *United States v. Bohle,* 1971). On the other hand, college and university officials might contend that they have an equally strong interest in upholding institutional standards, and in protecting the safety of others. Relying on the 1978 *Board of Curators* decision (which provided that formal hearings are not required for academic dismissals), campus administrators could assert that psychiatric withdrawals, like academic dismissals, "require . . . an expert evaluation of cumulative information" and are "not readily adapted to the procedural tools of judicial . . . decision-making" (*Board of Curators,* 1978, p. 90).

While it certainly would be prudent for college and university officials to refer to *Board of Curators,* a simplistic reliance upon the holding in that case would be unwise. The result, if not the reasoning, in *Board of Curators* was predictable, given the traditional reluctance of the judiciary to involve itself in *academic* decision-making. The psychiatric or psychological evaluation and removal of a student from a public college or university is a very different type of decision and would probably be viewed differently by the courts. This is so because the deference generally accorded to educators may not be sufficient to overcome the long standing judicial distrust of psychiatric labeling (see, e.g., Chief Justice Burger's views in *Addington,* 1979, p. 429). Given that distrust, *Board of Curators* can be readily distinguished on the ground that the psychiatric or psychological evaluation and withdrawal of a student is not a component of the normal student-teacher relationship. The student-teacher relationship in the college or university setting may require evaluation of academic performance, but it does not normally entail an official analysis of a student's "mental health." The latter is more akin to making a judgment about a person's character, and may be equally stigmatizing. Furthermore, the evaluation undertaken pursuant to a mandatory withdrawal procedure will often require the mental health professional, much as the disciplinarian depicted in *Goss* (1975), to "act on the reports . . . of others" (*Goss*, 1975, p. 580). This need for some sort of factual determination, coupled with the uncertainties of psychiatric diagnosis, and the dangers of psychiatric labeling, bring an inherent "adversary flavor" to the psychiatric withdrawal process which may result in the imposition of significant due process protections (see Justice Rhenquist's analysis in *Board of Curators*, 1978, p. 90.)

It is true that graduate or professional schools with clinical training programs can avoid psychiatric or disciplinary labeling by asserting that a student lacks the personal skills or qualities necessary for successful interaction with patients or clients. For example, it is not unreasonable to suggest that the *Board of Curators* case may have involved a "psychiatric withdrawal" by another name, given the fact that an apparently eccentric medical student was dismissed due to alleged deficiencies in "clinical competence, peer and patient relations, personal hygiene, and ability to accept criticism" (*Board of Curators*, 1978, p. 98). This approach is not without legal risks, however. Horowitz, the student in *Board of Curators*, was given a unique due process procedure (evaluation by an independent panel of physicians) which convinced even the most vigorous dissenter in the case that she had been accorded "as much procedural protection as the Due Process clause requires" (p. 103; Marshall, J., concurring in part and dissenting in part). The very nature of that independent evaluation required the evaluators to focus upon Horowitz's present clinical competency rather than her past conduct (p. 94, n.2). Other schools may be unwilling or unable to develop comparable procedural protections, and could be required by the courts to provide a traditional due process hearing if disputed facts are involved (see, e.g. *Brookins*, 1973).

Recent Court Decisions Requiring
Significant Due Process Protections

Most courts are likely to turn to sources other than the holding in *Board of Curators* to define the scope of due process protections when a student suffering from a mental disorder is subject to mandatory withdrawal at a public institution. The previously cited Supreme Court decisions in *Parham* and *Vitek*, while not directly relevant to the educational setting, will probably be regarded as offering at least some guidance.

As discussed earlier, the Supreme Court in *Parham* would require only minimal due process protections when parents or guardians seek admission of their minor children to state mental institutions. All that would be necessary would be "some kind of inquiry" by a "neutral factfinder," which "must also include an interview with the child" (pp. 606-607). A "quasi-formal hearing" conducted by "a law trained or a judicial or administrative officer" would be unnecessary, because, in part, it was to be presumed "that natural bonds of affection lead parents to act in the best interests of their children" (pp. 607 and 602). Moreover, although the Court "acknowledge[d] the fallibility of medical and psychiatric diagnosis" it did observe that "the supposed protections of an adversary proceeding to determine the appropriateness of medical decisions for the commitment and treatment of mental and emotional illness may well be more illusory than real" (p. 609).

Standing alone, a broad interpretation of the holding and reasoning in *Parham* would be dispositive of most of the procedural issues involved in the mandatory withdrawal of a student from a public college or university. Essentially, a school psychologist or psychiatrist could simply interview the student in question and render a professional "medical" diagnosis, resulting in summary withdrawal. However, less than nine months after the announcement of the decision in *Parham*, the Supreme Court dissenters in that case (Brennan, Marshall and Stevens) were joined by Justices White and Powell to form a new majority in *Vitek*. The Court then manifested a totally different attitude toward the procedural protections appropriate for certain types of "medical" inquiries conducted by the state. Borrowing from Chief Justice Burger's language in *Addington*, Justice White, writing for the majority, concluded that:

> [t]he question whether an individual is mentally ill . . . 'turns on the meaning of the facts which must be interpreted by expert psychiatrists and psychologists . . .' The medical nature of the inquiry, however, does not justify dispensing with due process requirements. It is precisely '(t)he subtleties and nuances of psychiatric diagnoses' that justify the requirement of adversary hearings (citation omitted) (p. 495).

The "due process requirements" outlined by the Court for the specific factual situation in *Vitek* (1980) included written notice, a hearing (in which the respondent could be heard in person, present witnesses, and, in most cases, cross examine opposing witnesses), an independent decision-maker (who could be from within the hospital administration), a written statement of findings, and competent representation, although not necessarily by a licensed attorney (*Vitek*, 1980, p. 497).

22

It is unclear whether all of the standard procedural protections set forth in *Vitek* would be fully and literally applied in the college and university setting. Nonetheless, both state and federal courts have recently indicated a willingness to impose significant due process requirements in cases involving psychiatric labeling and dismissal of public college and university students.* For example, in *Evans* (1980) the West Virginia Supreme Court ordered the immediate reinstatement of a student who had taken a leave of absence from a medical school while suffering "mental anguish" from a urological condition. The court held that if the school subsequently sought to dismiss the student, it would be necessary to provide various "due process protections," including a hearing, an opportunity to retain counsel, and "formal written notice of the reasons" for dismissal (pp. 780-781). Likewise, in *Nancy P.* (1981) a federal court in Indiana issued a temporary restraining order prohibiting the university from withdrawing a freshman who had attempted a suicide. The judge observed that "it appears . . . that the plaintiff may well have been deprived of due process rights . . . as it is questionable whether or not she was afforded an opportunity for an adequate hearing . . ." (p. 10). A similar lawsuit at the University of Massachusetts resulted in a preliminary finding against the University, and an out of court settlement (*Daily Collegian*, 1980).

It is becoming increasingly clear that the courts will require some form of due process proceeding before a public college or university student can be required to withdraw from school on mental health grounds. Nonetheless, since the law on the subject is not yet fully developed or articulated, there may still be an opportunity for colleges and universities to develop alternative policies which would accord students sufficient due process without replicating the procedural excesses frequently encountered in many campus disciplinary systems.

Suggested Procedural Protections for Mandatory Withdrawals

The Supreme Court has long recognized that "[t]he very nature of due process negates any concept of inflexible procedures universally applicable to every imaginable situation" (*Cafeteria Workers*, 1961, p. 895). Kenneth Culp Davis has observed that this procedural flexibility "should open a whole vista for imaginative procedural thinking of the kind that has been almost totally absent" (Davis, 1971, p. 228). Davis' comment is especially pertinent to the college and university setting, where the imposition of the traditional "contested

---

*Relevant litigation involving private schools is rare. In *Aronson* (1981) the court permitted a private school to rely upon a psychiatric withdrawal policy which was devoid of any due process protection, so long as there was no evidence of bad faith or malice. However, in *Tedeschi* (1980) an appellate court required the college to follow its disciplinary hearing procedures prior to dismissing a disruptive student who appeared to be suffering from a mental disorder. The requirements in both cases were based on a contractual relationship.

hearing" due process model simply is not the most effective and efficient way to accord substantial justice to students (see Kirp, 1976), especially those students subject to mandatory psychological or psychiatric withdrawal.

The primary defect with trial-type hearings in the college and university context is that they either create or intensify adversarial relationships between individuals who perceive themselves as belonging to an academic community. As a result, the more legalistic a respondent becomes or appears, the greater will be the threat which he or she is perceived to pose to the fundamental values of the institution. This problem probably would not be of great concern to most students, but for the painfully obvious (yet frequently overlooked) fact that those vested with the authority to resolve disputed cases will likely be distrustful of individuals who aggressively assert due process rights which are perceived to be alien to the educational process.

In the specific context of a mandatory psychological or psychiatric withdrawal, the ritualistic imposition of a trial-type hearing may satisfy a reviewing judge, but it probably will not be helpful to the student respondent, who is likely to be pitted in an adversarial battle with a subordinate of the individual who will ultimately resolve the case. For example, if a hearing is held before a Dean of Students, a Vice President for Student Affairs, or the like, a school psychologist or psychiatrist subjected to aggressive cross-examination by counsel in a formal hearing may soon be perceived as a sympathetic or even heroic figure, struggling to preserve cherished academic or professional values against the machinations of a predatory outsider. Except in extraordinary circumstances, the simple, practical result is that the decision of the mental health professional is almost certain to be upheld. Absent gross procedural error, lack of clear evidence, or some manifest form of invidious discrimination, the chances of successfully challenging such a final determination in the courts would be nil.

It is possible to conceive of legally acceptable alternatives to trial type proceedings which would be better suited to the academic community and offer substantial protection to students subject to involuntary withdrawal. Suggested guidelines are contained in the proposed "Standards and Procedures for Involuntary Withdrawal," set forth in Appendix I. The guidelines contain the following basic elements:

1. A clear statement of policy pertaining to involuntary withdrawal from the institution (or the residence halls) based upon a set of definitions for various mental disorders contained in the American Psychiatric Association *Diagnostic and Statistical Manual of Mental Disorders* (DSM-III, 1980). While DSM-III is not an acceptable document to all mental health professionals, it is the only viable alternative to ad hoc formulations which are likely to be even more vague and malleable. For example,

under a standard focusing on the student's "ability to adjust to campus life," an evaluator could readily discriminate on the ground of sexual preference. Such a result could not be so easily accomplished under a DSM-III standard, since homosexuality, per se, is not listed as a mental disorder.

2. The guidelines also require a showing that a student subject to involuntary withdrawal has engaged, or threatened to engage, in behavior which indicates that he or she poses a threat to self or others, may cause significant property damage, or directly and substantially impede the lawful activities of others. Furthermore, if the student has allegedly violated campus disciplinary regulations, the guidelines require that the case be resolved through the disciplinary process, unless the student lacks the capacity to respond to the charges, or did not know the nature or wrongfulness of the act in question.

3. Adequate advance notice is given to the student that he or she may be subject to involuntary withdrawal. Prior notice and hearing need not be accorded in "emergency" situations, but should follow as soon as possible (see *Goss*, 1978, pp. 582-83).

4. Whenever possible, a lay administrative officer will rely upon an independent evaluation prepared by a mental health professional not affiliated with the institution.

5. An opportunity is given to the student to examine the evaluation and to discuss it in an informal proceeding with the campus administrative officer before any final determination is made. The student might be assisted by a family member, and by a mental health professional of his or her choice. Although some mental health professionals may not want to disclose a diagnosis to a student in this setting, that consideration must be balanced against the risk (and public perception) that students may be withdrawn and stigmatized on the basis of secret and perhaps erroneous information. One example of a comparable requirement in state involuntary commitment proceedings is the 1976 Pennsylvania Mental Health Procedures Act (Pa. Stat. Ann. tit. 50, 7101-7503, Purdon Supp. 1980) which requires (at 7303) an "informal hearing" in which the respondent may hear an explanation of the psychiatrist's finding "in terms understandable to a layman." See also *Rennie* (1981). In any event, substantial numbers of mental health professionals would permit access to diagnostic information in similar proceedings (Kahle and Sales, 1978).

6. Instead of active participation by legal counsel, a tenured faculty member from an appropriate discipline should be assigned to interview the student and to appear at the proceeding for the express purpose of questioning and challenging the withdrawal recommendation. The faculty member should not be considered the student's "representative," but, much as the "Devil's Advocate" in canon law, an advocate for the institution's interest in avoiding an erroneous determination.

7. A statement of reasons should be given for any decision requiring a student to withdraw from school on mental health grounds (see *Evans*, 1980).

These suggested due process guidelines might obviate the need for more formal proceedings, since the grounds for psychiatric withdrawal are narrowly defined, and because provision is made for an independent evaluation of the student's behavior.* The use of some form of independent evaluation appeared to be an important consideration for the Supreme Court in the *Board of Curators* case, and has been referred to elsewhere as a possible component of procedural fairness in cases involving psychiatric decision-making (*Rennie*, 1981). Furthermore, the student, and a person assisting him, could meet with a lay administrator responsible for reviewing the evaluation, and would be able to challenge any factual errors or inaccurate assumptions contained therein.

The proposed guidelines also meet the requirements of Section 504 of the Rehabilitation Act of 1973, and provide that the institution could not simply rely upon a diagnosis of mental illness in order to withdraw a student. Instead, certain forms of overt behavior, or threats of such behavior, would be required. This standard is similar to what some courts have mandated in involuntary commitment cases. For example, in *Lynch* (1974) a Federal district court held that "[a] mere expectancy that danger productive behavior might be engaged in" is not sufficient. Instead, "it must be shown that [the individual] has actually been dangerous in the recent past and that such danger was manifested by an overt act, attempt or threat to do substantial harm to himself or to another" (p. 391).

Perhaps the most unusual ingredient in the suggested guidelines is the participation of a tenured faculty member assigned to question any recommendation that a student be withdrawn on mental health grounds. The use of such a "devil's advocate" has a long history in the evolution of techniques to check administrative power, and could be especially effective in the school setting, given the existence of a tenure system. That system offers an opportunity for procedural innovation in this context, because a competent faculty member with appropriate training and at least some degree of job security can be expected to ask intelligent questions about an involuntary withdrawal recommendation in a way which might be credible to the decision-maker. Also, since the faculty member would not be "representing" the student, it might be possible to avoid the defensive reaction which could be engendered by legal counsel in an adversary proceeding. This

---

*The University of Virginia recently developed a comprehensive psychiatric withdrawal policy providing for hearing panel participation by "a psychiatrist who is not employed at the University's Student Health Services . . ." (*Procedures*, p. 4).

26

technique is certainly not a panacea, and will be subject to abuse on some campuses. On balance, however, more students are likely to receive careful consideration through such a process than in traditional due process hearings.

Due Process Summary

Administrators at public colleges and universities can expect that they will be required to accord some sort of due process protection to students subject to mandatory psychological or psychiatric withdrawal. This is so because the stigma associated with psychiatric labeling is intrinsically damaging and dehumanizing, thereby constituting a deprivation of "liberty," as defined by the courts. Private schools may also wish to offer comparable protections to students, both on the grounds of simple fairness, and because such safeguards might prevent reliance upon the "incorrect [factual] assumptions" (*Pushkin*, 1981, p. 1383) which could cause either public or private institutions to run afoul of Section 504 of the Rehabilitation Act of 1973. In any event, the academic community may still have sufficient time to develop efficient and equitable withdrawal policies which might forestall the judicial imposition of more onerous, and probably less effective, procedural requirements. A sample policy, which would need to be modified and adapted for the needs of individual campuses, is set forth in Appendix I.

Chapter IV

Policy Considerations in Mandatory Withdrawals

The fact that a properly drafted psychiatric withdrawal policy might withstand legal challenge does not mean that campus officials should readily resort to it. A reliance upon campus disciplinary regulations, or state psychiatric commitment procedures, will often be a better alternative for students, the campus, and for the surrounding community as well (see, generally, Tanner and Sewell, 1979; Gehring, 1983). Essentially, the resort to a mandatory psychiatric withdrawal in any specific case should be undertaken with extreme care, and only after other reasonable alternatives have been considered. Several such policy considerations are explored in this chapter.

LIABILITY FOR FAILING TO PROTECT

Perhaps the greatest single inducement to the hasty reliance upon psychiatric withdrawal policies on campuses across the country has been the fear of tort liability for failing to protect students from the violent acts of others, or from their own self-destructive behavior. Unfortunately, educators are frequently confused about relevant case law, and have often formed distorted impressions based upon stories in the popular press, or "word of mouth" accounts from their colleagues. More often than not, those impressions dramatically overstate the legal risks entailed in failing to predict and prevent violence on campus.

It is true that an educational institution would be vulnerable for failing to take reasonable measures to protect a student from a foreseeable assault.* For example, in 1980, the Arizona Supreme Court

---

*Readers should be alerted to a new case now pending before the New York State Supreme Court Appellate Division - Fourth Department. In *Eiseman* (1983), a lower court found the State University of New York - College at Buffalo (SUCB)

held that a college might be held liable when a campus security guard failed to heed the victim's repeated warnings of an imminent assault specifically threatened by a previously identified assailant (*Jesik*, 1980). Likewise, in *Tarasoff II* (1976) the California Supreme Court held that university psychiatrists could be held liable for failing to take reasonable care to warn a readily identifiable victim whom their client had threatened to harm. (See also, *McIntosh*, 1979). Finally, in *Mullins* (1983), a state court in Massachusetts held that a college near a large metropolitan area had a duty to provide reasonable physical security for students living in the residence halls. The court noted that the college itself had "actually foreseen" the risk of criminal acts by outsiders on campus, but lacked adequate security equipment and procedures (p. 337; see also *Miller*, 1984; *Peterson*, 1984).

The fact that educational institutions owe certain legal duties to students does not mean that college and university officials must somehow guarantee the safety of every member of the academic community, including those who might be injured by a student suffering from a mental disorder. Instead, in many jurisdictions, judges have reiterated that a campus official is "not required to take precautions against a sudden attack from a third person which he has no reason to anticipate" (*Relyea*, 1980, p. 1383). Basically, courts recognize that educators simply cannot protect students from those types of "spontaneous" or "unprovoked acts of violence" which "even the most sophisticated security forces are powerless to prevent" (*Hall*, 1981, p. 1126; see also *Setrin*, 1975; and *Brown*, 1983).

---

liable for the off-campus rape and murder of a student (Rhona Eiseman) by another student (Larry Campbell), who applied to SUCB while incarcerated on felony drug charges. Campbell had a long history of violent behavior, and was previously diagnosed as "a paranoid-schizophrenic drug addict with a belligerent personality and little likelihood of rehabilitation" (Amicus Brief of American Council on Education, p. 5). The court determined that the University owed a duty to protect other students from unreasonable harm, and that the decision to admit Campbell (who, inexplicably, was also allowed to live in the residence halls) was negligent. Specific acts of negligence, as identified by the court, included a failure by SUCB to inquire about Campbell's mental health history, or to conduct its own psychiatric evaluation; acceptance of letters of evaluation from individuals "incapable of providing the type of knowledgable, dispassionate character evaluation its own application form sought and common sense required;" and failure to consider Campbell's known status as an incarcerated felon and to conduct "more than its usual inquiry into [his] personal background" (opinion, p. 65). In short, the court concluded that "[h]ad SUCB inquired into Campbell's background . . . prudence, diligence, and common sense would have intervened to prevent [his] admission, or at the very least, to have so restricted his activities as to minimize the risk of harm to other students, faculty, and staff . . . .[The fact] that Campbell's rampage was foreseeable is all too apparent from his prior record of which SUCB chose to remain ignorant" (opinion, pp. 67-68). *(The author is indebted to the General Counsel's office, State University of New York, and to Mr. Eugene D. Gulland, of the law firm of Covington and Burling in Washington, D.C., for providing the unreported lower court opinion and amicus brief in this case).*

Foreseeable Danger and Foreseeable Victim

The determination of institutional liability in the aftermath of third party criminal behavior depends upon the issue of "foreseeability." It certainly is clear that liability might be imposed if a counselor failed to warn an individual who could be readily identified as a potential victim of the counselor's client.* Even the very strict confidentiality requirements of the various mental health professions would permit such a warning (*McIntosh*, 1979, p. 512-513; Stone, 1976, p. 374; Fleming and Maximov, 1974, p. 1032; American Psychological Association, 1981, p. 4; American Psychiatric Association, 1975, p. 13). Also, it has been established that those who administer medical institutions offering psychiatric treatment may be held responsible for failing to exercise reasonable care in retaining custody of a patient (*Underwood*, 1966; *Semler*, 1976; *Lipari*, 1981; *Petersen*, 1983). However, in the absence of a manifest threat, or a pattern of violent behavior in the past (see *Johnson*, 1968; *Eiseman*, 1983), it is unlikely that campus officials or mental health professionals would be expected to determine whether a student suffering from a mental disorder might harm someone in the future.

Most knowledgeable observers are increasingly aware of the difficulties involved in attempting to predict the future behavior of a person suffering from a mental disorder (Cocozza and Steadman, 1978; Kahle and Sales, 1978; Dershowitz, 1970). It is probably for this reason that many courts limit the "duty to warn" to those situations in which the prospective victim is readily identifiable (*Leedy*, 1981). Even the California Supreme Court, which set forth the liability standard in *Tarasoff II*, reiterated in *Thompson* (1980) that a mental health professional has no "*general* duty to warn of each threat." Instead, liability would be imposed only if the victim was "the known and specifically foreseeable and identifiable" target "of the patient's threats" (p. 734, emphasis in original). This position was recently adopted by an appellate court in Michigan, which observed that:

> . . . a psychiatrist will not be held liable for his patient's violent behavior simply because he failed to predict it accurately . . . . To require a psychiatrist to use due care to protect another whenever he encounters the slightest hint that his patient might endanger that person would be an intolerable burden (*Davis*, 1983, pp. 484, 488).

A few relevant decisions have not been as restrictive as *Leedy*, *Thompson*, or *Davis*, and have suggested that the relationship between a mental health professional and patient gives rise to an affirmative duty to third persons who may not be readily identifiable (*Lipari*, 1981, pp. 193-194). Nonetheless, holdings of this nature may

---

*It will be important to review the law of each state. For example, in Maryland, a 1980 opinion seems to suggest that such a warning would violate a statutory privilege belonging to the patient. See *Shaw* (1980).

not produce a significantly different result, since at least some courts base the liability standard upon the prevailing "standards of [the mental health] profession" in determining whether a "patient's dangerous propensities present an unreasonable risk of harm to others" (*Lipari*, 1981, p. 193). Those standards, as set forth in the professional literature, indicate that mental health professionals cannot reliably predict dangerousness in an individual who has not acted in a dangerous way. For example, the American Psychiatric Association has stated that attempting to predict future behavior "gives the appearance of being based on expert medical judgment, when in fact no such expertise exists" (American Psychiatric Association, 1981, p. 5). An American Psychological Association Task Force reached the same conclusion in 1978, and reported that "the validity of psychological predictions of dangerous behavior . . . is extremely poor, so poor that one could oppose their use on the strictly empirical grounds that psychologists are not professionally competent to make such judgments" (American Psychological Association Task Force, 1978, p. 30).

A national consensus on a liability standard for the "duty to warn" simply has not evolved. At one extreme, the broad language contained in the *Lipari* opinion represents a position which may significantly disrupt the confidential relationship between a therapist and a patient. From the opposite viewpoint, Alan Stone, Professor of Law and Psychiatry at Harvard University, has argued that liability should be imposed "only at the point at which the therapist has formed his judgment" and "decided that his patient is dangerous . . ." (Stone, 1976, p. 375). This standard, of course, would all but preclude successful litigation against mental health professionals, unless a therapist was consciously indifferent to the safety of others. In the middle of these two positions is the formulation set forth in *Thompson*. It is the standard most likely to be adopted in the majority of jurisdictions, because it is comparatively precise and objective, and would result in the most careful balance between the reasonable requirements of mental health professionals, and the need to protect the public. Also, taken literally, the language in *Thompson* is especially valuable because it appears to resolve the troublesome question of whether or not a prudent therapist should automatically warn appropriate third parties about any violent "fantasies" expressed by a patient. By limiting the reporting requirement to "threats" which pose a "serious danger" to a foreseeable victim, the court in *Thompson* sought to protect the "open and confidential character of psychotherapeutic dialogue . . ." (pp. 734, 752, citing *Tarasoff II*), and the social benefits which presumably result therefrom.

The Duty to Control Student Behavior

The *Thompson* standard has considerable potential to diminish many of the concerns expressed by mental health professionals.

Furthermore, counselors and administrators at colleges and universities should also be aware of important case law which has recognized that college students have acquired expanded rights to privacy and autonomy in recent years, and that it has become increasingly difficult for campus officials to monitor and control student behavior. In *Bradshaw* (1979), a federal appeals court held that a college did not owe a duty of care to a student injured in an automobile driven by an underage fellow student, who was apparently under the influence of alcohol. Both students had been participants in an unsupervised, off-campus, sophomore class picnic at which alcohol had been served. The alcohol had been purchased with class funds through a check co-signed by a faculty member, who also participated in planning the affair. Flyers announcing the picnic (featuring drawings of beer mugs) were then duplicated at the college and widely distributed on campus. Not suprisingly, the injured student contended that the college failed to enforce its own regulations pertaining to underage drinking, and had a duty to control the behavior of the students participating in the class picnic. The court disagreed, holding that "the modern American college is not an insurer of the safety of its students," (p. 138) and observed:

> [t]here was a time when college administrators . . . assumed a role *in loco parentis* . . . A special relationship was created between college and student that imposed a duty on the college to exercise control over student conduct and, reciprocally, gave the students certain rights of protection by the college. The campus revolutions of the late sixties . . . produced fundamental changes . . . Regulation by the college of student life on and off campus has become limited . . . Under these circumstances, we think it would be placing an impossible burden on the college to impose a duty in this case (pp. 139, 140, 142).

Although the *Bradshaw* case has been followed in other jurisdictions (see *Baldwin*, 1981), it should not lead to complacency, or be misread to mean that colleges may routinely ignore persistent violations of campus policies. Nonetheless, the rationale in *Bradshaw*, coupled with the carefully circumscribed "duty to warn" defined in *Thompson*, indicates that the courts have not been inclined to place onerous or unreasonable burdens on institutions to protect students from the negligence or criminal behavior of others. Colleges are simply not being asked to assume responsibilities which the larger society is unable to fulfill, or which, if imposed on campus, could lead to repressive measures destructive to the values of tolerance and diversity in the academic community.

Liability For Suicides

Many educators are also fearful that they may be held liable if a student commits suicide on campus. As a result, they are frequently tempted to invoke mandatory withdrawal procedures whenever a student manifests any self-destructive behavior. This practice is based upon a misunderstanding of the law, and may not be helpful to the student (see analysis at p. 57). Moreover, to the extent that campus officials simply withdraw suicidal students — without attempting to secure immediate treatment for them — the reliance upon a mandatory withdrawal policy may actually increase the risk of liability.

Cases in which third parties are held legally responsible either for failing to prevent or for causing the suicidal behavior of others are extremely rare. This is so because the decision to commit suicide is often unforeseeable (Kahle and Sales, 1978, p. 435) and because it is viewed as a "superseding cause" of death which cannot fairly be attributed to most defendants (*Maricopa County*, 1970, p. 267). Even for institutions such as hospitals, the courts have recognized "the difficulty of preventing suicide" and are "reluctant to impose . . . liability in all but the most egregious circumstances" (Braunstein, 1982, p. 200).

The "egregious circumstances" resulting in recovery generally involve custodial settings (i.e., a confined person is dependent upon the institution for care) in which institutional officials have ignored prior specific suicide threats or attempts (*Smith*, 1977). Also, liability may be imposed in certain other unusual situations, such as a hotel in which the upper floors became "an attractive location for suicides, in light of the prior history of suicide . . . in the hotel" (*Sneider*, 1975, p. 978). Finally, it is possible that a mental health professional could be held liable for failing to arrange emergency psychiatric treatment for a patient who had attempted suicide, or had articulated a credible suicide threat (see "Note," 1961, p. 520; Greenberg, 1974).

In the educational environment, courts have endorsed the observation that "as a particular relationship fails to resemble the caretaking relationship of hospital toward patient, it becomes less likely that the person in a superior position will be able to recognize another's suicidal tendencies" (Knuth, 1979, p. 992; see *Bogust*, 1960). Contrary to the impressions which one might draw from the average faculty meeting, educational institutions are distinctly different from mental hospitals, at least in their capacity to effectively supervise and control a resident population (see, generally, *Figueroa*, 1980). Above all, a college or university will not be considered "an insurer of its pupil's mental health" (*Wilson*, 1979, p. 684).

Ironically, one of the greatest risks of liability in the aftermath of suicidal behavior by a student would be the automatic resort to a mandatory withdrawal policy. The professional and ethical obligations of a trained counselor or therapist on campus would preclude any practice of simply "dumping" a suicidal individual in the larger society. Instead, at least in most cases of attempted suicide, the generally accepted standard of professional conduct would be referral for emergency psychiatric evaluation, including involuntary commitment, if necessary. It certainly might be possible under these circumstances to initiate prompt intervention and treatment, without the potentially harmful result of removing the student from school altogether.

Liability Summary

Educators often overstate the risk of liability for failing to protect students from the violent acts of others, or from self-destructive behavior. It is true that liability may result if dangerous conditions are tolerated, reasonable security devices not installed or maintained, habitual and dangerous misbehavior disregarded, or threats of violence ignored. Nonetheless, courts have not held that college and university officials must somehow guarantee the safety of every member of the academic community, or serve as an insurer of their mental health. Generally, in the absence of a manifest threat, or a pattern of violent behavior in the past, it is unlikely that campus administrators would be expected to determine whether any student (including a student suffering from a mental disorder) might harm themselves or others.

Over-Prediction of Dangerousness

Mental health professionals do not appear to be able to predict violent behavior with any significant degree of reliability. Thus, it would be unreasonable for administrators to expect them to determine whether a student suffering from an apparent "emotional problem" might constitute a danger to self or others. When such expectations are imposed on psychiatrists and psychologists, it is more likely than not that dangerousness will be over-predicted. This means that many students who are withdrawn on mental health grounds may be erroneously stigmatized and removed from school.

There is a great temptation to assume that a student suffering from a particular mental disorder must pose a substantial threat of violence. Dr. Steven S. Sharfstein, Deputy Medical Director of the American Psychiatric Association, has challenged that assumption, and observed that:

> . . . mental illness, like many other diseases, affects each individual differently. A particular mental illness does not automatically give rise to a specific behavior. Very few persons diagnosed as depressed commit suicide; very few persons diagnosed a schizophrenic become violent. Psychiatrists cannot predict future violence any more than other practitioners can predict whether their patients suddenly will develop an allergy to a medication they have taken throughout their lives (Sharfstein, 1983, p. A18).

Similarly, another prominent psychiatrist has observed that even individuals with "violent fantasies" are not necessarily dangerous, since "some of the patients who have the most violent fantasies are statistically the least likely to carry them out" (Restak, 1983, p. A25).

The burdens which may have been placed on mental health professionals to predict violent behavior were probably premised upon an assumption that there is a connection between violence and mental disorders. Significantly, however, recent studies have shown that there is "no general relationship between crime and mental illness" (Bower, 1984, p. 367; see also Ennis and Litwack, 1974, p. 716). Indeed, Dr. Bernard Diamond has cited research showing "a lesser involvement in criminal behavior by the mentally ill than is true for the general population" (Diamond, 1974, p. 448). In short, while persons with mental disorders certainly may commit crimes, the most likely predictor of future criminal behavior is not mental illness, but a pattern of crime in the past.

Many administrators still assume that a student who is apparently suffering from a mental disorder must pose a danger to self or others. Having formed that predilection, they may turn to a campus mental health professional for an authoritative evaluation and confirmation. This process will very likely produce the result originally anticipated by the administrator, since the psychologist or psychiatrist has much to gain and very little to lose by recommending the student's dismissal. Such a recommendation generally enhances the power and authority of the person making it, and has the additional benefit of confirming what is likely to be the unspoken assumption of an administrative superior. Overcaution in these matters also has the value of being empirically unverifiable (i.e., the dismissed student has left the campus and is in a different environment), while a contrary determination will always be subject to challenge if the student should engage in prohibited behavior at any time in the future.

The simple fact is that many mental health professionals have responded favorably to inducements to over-predict violence. In one famous example, 121 persons determined to be "dangerous criminally insane" in New York state were ordered released on the ground that the state commitment procedure was unconstitutional. A subsequent study revealed that "[i]n the four years following release, this group accounted for only sixteen criminal convictions involving no more than nine individuals—a rate which is not appreciably higher, if at all, than that expected in a random sample of normal persons." Furthermore, only 2.7% of the entire group were returned to New York hospitals for the criminally insane (Fleming and Maximov, 1974, p. 1044). Other knowledgeable observers who have studied this phenomenon also conclude that "psychiatrists who make such judgments tend to over-predict dangerousness greatly, by a factor somewhere between ten and a hundred times the actual incidence of dangerous behavior" (Diamond, 1974, p. 447; see also Rubin, 1972, and Dershowitz, 1970).

It is important to emphasize at this point that nothing said here is designed to convey an impression that colleges and universities must ignore the safety of the campus community. Students who engage in violence, or who threaten to do so, should be subject to strict disciplinary action, including immediate suspension from the institution (see Pavela, 1980, p. 43). As will be discussed in detail later, it has been the apparent reluctance of many campus administrators to impose a just punishment in serious disciplinary cases which has encouraged the hasty reliance upon mandatory withdrawal procedures in order to dismiss apparently dangerous students. A major advantage of the disciplinary process is that such institutional action would not be based upon unreliable predictions of future conduct. Instead, it would have to be shown the individual has engaged in *overt behavior* (i.e., an act, attempt, or threat) which posed a danger to others. (See, generally, *Lynch*, 1974, for "overt act" requirement in involuntary commitment cases).This standard is designed to offer substantial protection to the community, while safeguarding the legitimate interests of students who might appear to be eccentric or "strange," and therefore "dangerous."

The Potential for Bias in Psychological/Psychiatric Evaluation

When asked to determine if a student is "mentally ill" and "dangerous" it is questionable whether mental health professionals can form any kind of a scientifically valid conclusion based upon the brief evaluative interview required in many mandatory withdrawal policies. Karl Menninger has been especially critical of the legal profession for its expectations in this regard:

[m]ost lawyers have no conception of the meaning or methods of psychiatric case study and diagnosis. They seem to think that psychiatrists can take a quick look at a suspect . . . and thereupon be able to say, definitely, that the awful 'it' . . . the loathsome affliction of 'insanity' . . . is present or absent. Because we all like to please, some timid psychiatrists fall in with this fallacy of the lawyers and go through these preposterous antics (Menninger, 1959, pp. 137-38).

The unwillingness of "timid" psychiatrists and psychologists to recognize the limits of their expertise dramatically increases the chances that mandatory withdrawal policies may be intentionally or unintentionally misused by mental health professionals to impose their own social or moral values on campus. This was a special concern of the American Psychological Association Board of Social and Ethical Responsibility for Psychology, which issued a report in 1978 stating that the practice of expecting mental health professionals to identify "dangerous" individuals results in the professional "imposing his or her values as to the degree of risk society should bear" (American Psychological Association, 1978, p. 19). Moreover, several studies have shown that such diagnoses are also influenced by factors such as a client's social class (Gross, 1978, p. 51; see also Torry, 1974, pp. 46-52), or cultural background (Ennis and Litwack, 1974, p. 725; Adebimpe, 1981), or even by the "political predilections" of the diagnostician (Kress, 1979, p. 217).

Most of us recognize that mental health professionals—as all human beings—have biases which should be challenged. Nonetheless, psychiatrists and psychologists are occasionally permitted to exercise unquestioned authority in a society which appears anxious to find a new "scientific standard of behavior" in order to replace a traditional religious perspective (Gross, 1978, p. 4). Perhaps the most grotesque example of such an attitude occured in Long Island in 1981. Several married women received anonymous telephone calls from an individual purporting to be a psychiatrist. The man claimed he was treating their husbands for "deep seated sexual problems" and that the "treatment" required the women to have sex with strangers. Obediently following orders, the women summoned men from the streets in front of their homes and performed sexual acts with them while the "psychiatrist" listened on the telephone (*Washington Post*, October 2, 1981, p. A9).

Hopefully, most college and university officials would not be as acquiescent as the victims of the pseudo-psychiatrist in Long Island. Nonetheless, the danger remains that administrators may be inclined to grant too much discretionary authority to mental health professionals. Such a practice could inhibit healthy forms of diversity and social experimentation on campus, especially if one accepts the possibility that "[p]eople who now become analysts and therapists are apt to be cautious careerists, uncritical supporters of adjustment to conventional values and norms" (LaBier, 1983, p. C5). This risk is not insignificant, given the fact that there is at least some evidence of a link between intense creativity and certain mood disorders (*New York Times*, Sept. 23, 1984, p. 63). Indeed, there has been a long history of psychiatric analysis which belittled precisely those forms of creative genius which should be fostered in the academic community. This was the point made by Viktor E. Frankl, when he cited a book review critical of a two volume Freudian analysis of Goethe:

> [i]n the 1538 pages, the author portrays to us a genius with the earmarks of a manic-depressive, paranoid, and epileptoid disorder, of homosexuality, incest, voyeurism, exhibitionism, fetishism, impotence, narcissism, obsessive-compulsive neurosis, hysteria, megalomania, etc. The author seems to focus exclusively upon the instinctual dynamic forces that underlie the artistic product. We are led to believe that Goethe's work is but the result of pregenital fixations. His struggle does not really aim for an ideal, for beauty, for values, but for the overcoming of an embarrassing problem of premature ejaculation (Frankl, 1978, p. 88).

Even if it were possible to avoid social, cultural, or political biases in psychiatric evaluation, campus administrators should be aware that there is strong evidence which suggests that "being a mental health professional may constitute a set to perceive mental illness. . ." (Temerlin, 1970, p. 115; Gaylin, 1982, p. 286). This is not to be regarded as unusual, since psychiatrists, as most physicians, "tend to err on the side of medical caution. . ." (*Parham*, 1979, p. 629). Nonetheless, as one commentator has observed, "what holds true for medicine does not hold equally well for psychiatry. Medical illnesses, while unfortunate, are not commonly pejorative. Psychiatric diagnoses, on the contrary, carry with them personal, legal and social stigmas . . ." (Rosenhan, 1973, p. 252) which can have devastating consequences.

Appropriate Assistance of Mental Health Professionals

A recognition of present limitations in the practice of psychiatry or psychology does not mean that mental health professionals are unable to render any assistance when a determination concerning the possible mandatory withdrawal of a student must be made. In the broadest sense, such assistance might include:

1. Careful evaluation of a student to determine if the student may be suffering from a specifically defined mental disorder. Students should be informed in advance that the evaluation is not part of a confidential, therapeutic relationship;

2. Prudent questioning by a mental health professional in the evaluation process might elicit a history of violent behavior by the student, and what stresses, if any, contributed to that behavior. Furthermore, students may make specific threats of violence in the course of the evaluation, including plans or preparations to harm themselves. These are precisely the types of information which most mental health professionals use in order to determine a patient's potential for violence (Bower, 1984, p 367);

3. Finally, it seems reasonable to suggest that experienced and capable mental health professionals "are almost certain to possess a gift of insight which is unaccounted for by their technical apparatus" (Lippmann, 1929, p. 173). While it would be unwise to regard such insights as being "scientific" in nature, they should not be disregarded altogether.

The final decision concerning the possible mandatory withdrawal of a student is normally made by an administrative officer. Like a judge in a criminal case, the administrator must rely upon "[i]mpressions about an individual . . . the likelihood that he will transgress no more, the hope that he may respond to rehabilitative efforts . . . the degree to which he does or does not deem himself at war with his society . . ." (*United States*, 1978, p. 51). These "impressions" can and should be based on common sense assessments, derived not only from the administrator's observations, but from the information and insights offered by qualified mental health professionals.

Diagnosis and Prediction of Dangerousness—Summary

Essentially, psychiatry and psychology appear to be more akin to an art than a science. Such an art is usually practiced in the context of individual therapy on a voluntary basis, and, in the words of a recent American Psychological Association report, is not well suited for use "as a means to pursue administrative ends. . . ." (Task Force Report, 1978, p. 10). There may be occasions when an administrator may wish to obtain an evaluation of a student by a mental health professional. Such an evaluation could provide new and valuable insights into the student's behavior. The final decision, however, should not be based upon unrealistic expectations of the current capabilities of mental health professionals, and must always be tempered by an awareness of the damaging stigma associated with a finding of mental illness.

Chapter V

The Benefits of Discipline

The psychiatric withdrawal of a student, based solely on a finding that the student was suffering from a mental disorder, would be precluded by Section 504 of the Rehabilitation Act of 1973. Accordingly, the focus of inquiry in any psychiatric withdrawal procedure must be on specific, usually prohibited behavior, which indicates that the student poses a physical threat to self or to others, or is otherwise unable to meet reasonable institutional standards. With very few exceptions, these are precisely the forms of behavior which campus disciplinary systems should be designed to address.

AVOIDING PROCEDURALISM

Some administrators may be inclined to rely on psychiatric withdrawal policies largely because the disciplinary systems on their campuses have become "mired in legalistic disputes over rules of evidence" (Lamont, 1979, p. 85). Part of the responsibility for this problem rests with college and university attorneys, who apparently failed to explain to campus officials that court cases setting forth "due process" requirements at public institutions never mandated the full-blown adversarial hearings now found at many colleges and universities. Lacking proper legal advice, or succumbing to student pressure, educational administrators turned instinctively to the criminal justice model for guidance, and developed extraordinarily complex judicial systems, some requiring unanimous verdicts, multiple appeals, the "beyond a reasonable doubt" standard of proof and the like. As a result, most schools now face a greater risk of being sued for running afoul of their own convoluted regulations (see e.g. *Tedeschi*, 1980; *Marshall*, 1980) than for violating the simple standards of "basic fairness" which the judiciary required.

A better understanding of the due process requirements in student disciplinary cases should begin with the concept that the amount of due process should be in proportion to the penalty which might be imposed. For example, a student accused of participating in a minor prank in a residence hall might be in jeopardy of being placed on residence hall probation, required to make a small contribution to a local charity, or complete a campus service project. All the due process that would be necessary under these circumstances would be "oral or written notice of the charges against him and, if he denies them, an explanation of the evidence that authorities have and an opportunity to present his side of the story" in an informal "discussion" with a school official (*Goss*, 1975, p. 581).* The rationale for this common sense approach was best expressed by a federal judge in Kentucky, who recently observed that if educators have to make "a federal case out of every petty disciplinary incident, the whole purpose of having any discipline at all and any rules of conduct would be defeated" (*Bahr*, 1982, p. 487).

The basic due process protections which are required in more serious disciplinary cases at public institutions have been outlined in holdings such as *Dixon* (1961), *Esteban* (1967), *Morale* (1976) a Missouri federal court "General Order" (1968), and in *Sohmer* (1982). Even in these cases, however, a formal, adversarial hearing has not been required. Most recently, in *Moresco* (1984) a New York State appellate court reiterated that:

> [p]etitioner was served with a written notice of charges; she was made aware of grounds which would justify her expulsion or suspension by way of the student handbook; the hearing tribunal afforded her an opportunity to hear and confront the evidence presented against her and an opportunity to be heard and to offer other evidence if she chose; she was accorded the right to have someone from the college community to assist her in the proceedings; she was informed of the tribunal's finding; she was given access to its decision for her personal review; and, finally, she was advised in writing of the discipline imposed. We find that this procedure adequately satisfied due process requirements in a collegial atmosphere (p. 4).

Likewise, the more detailed procedural guidelines specified by the courts for hearings in serious disciplinary cases are not onerous, and can be outlined as follows:

1. Students subject to disciplinary sanctions are entitled to a written statement of charges. Furthermore, accused students should be given the names of potential witnesses against them, and be informed of the nature of the witnesses' proposed testimony (*Wright*, 1968; *Sohmer*, 1982). Also, before any hearing or conference, students should be allowed to examine any written

---

*A number of colleges and universities do not conduct formal hearings in minor cases. Instead, students are informed that the charges will be resolved in a disciplinary conference with an administrative officer. See, e.g., the University of Colorado *Standards of Conduct*, p. 10 (1984-85).

evidence or exhibits which the institution plans to submit (*Esteban*, 1967).

2. Students who are entitled to a hearing should be informed of the hearing date, time, and location, and should be given reasonable time to prepare a defense. One court has suggested that ten days notice would be sufficient (*Speake*, 1970). Also, absent a showing of prejudice, more than one charge against a student can be considered at a hearing (*Turof*, 1981). Students who pose an immediate threat to others may be subject to an interim suspension prior to the hearing (*Goss*, 1975).

3. A hearing may be conducted in the absence of a student who fails to appear after campus officials have made a reasonable effort to provide adequate advance notice of the hearing time, date, and location (*Wright*, 1968).

4. The Family Educational Rights and Privacy Act (20 U.S.C. 1232(g)) would preclude holding an "open" hearing without the consent of the accused student (*correspondence to author from Department of Education, November 20, 1981*). It might be sound policy to permit an open hearing if the student so requests, but at least one court has indicated that there is no constitutional right to an open disciplinary hearing in the educational setting (*Hart*, 1983).

5. Hearings need not be delayed until after a student has been tried on any concurrent criminal charges (*Goldberg*, 1967; *Nzuve*, 1975; *Hart*, 1983).

6. A reasonable effort should be made to accommodate the schedule of any representative or advisor allowed to assist the accused student. For example, if campus rules permit legal representation, an attorney who affirms that he or she must appear in court at the same time as the disciplinary hearing should be given a continuance. Nonetheless, hearing officers retain broad discretion in granting continuances, and need not permit attorneys or others to delay disciplinary proceedings without compelling justification (see *Morris*, 1983).

7. None of the cases setting forth general due process requirements has indicated that students must be appointed to serve on disciplinary hearing panels (*Winnick*, 1972). Nonetheless, many schools elect to do so as a matter of policy. Establishment of a racial quota for membership on judicial panels at public institutions might be unconstitutional (*Uzzell*, 1984).

8. Individuals serving on disciplinary hearing panels need not be disqualified because they have a superficial knowledge of the background of the case, or because they may know the participants. The basic test is whether or not the panelists can "judge the case fairly and solely on the evidence presented . . ." (*Keene*, 1970, p. 222; see also *Wasson*, 1967; *Jones*, 1968; and *Blanton*, 1973). However, hearing panelists should not have participated in investigating or prosecuting the case (*Marshall*, 1980).

9. The "beyond a reasonable doubt" standard of proof used in criminal cases need not be adopted in campus disciplinary proceedings. Instead, at least one court has held that a student's guilt should be established by "clear and convincing evidence" (*Smyth*, 1975, p. 799).

10. Circumstantial evidence may be used in criminal proceedings and in campus disciplinary cases (*McDonald*, 1974). Likewise, colleges are not required to exclude "hearsay" evidence, although it would be unwise to base a finding of guilt on hearsay evidence alone. Most other technical rules of evidence are not applicable in campus disciplinary proceedings (*Goldberg*, 1967).

11. Students appearing before disciplinary panels may be directed to answer questions pertaining to the charges against them. Students who refuse to answer on the ground of the Fifth Amendment privilege may be informed that the hearing panel could draw negative inferences from their refusal which might result in the imposition of significant disciplinary sanctions. Several courts have held that the response of a student who then elected to answer could not be used against him in a criminal proceeding (*Goldberg*, 1967; *Furutani*, 1969, *Nzuve*, 1975; *Hart*, 1983).

12. Most courts have held that students have no due process right to representation by legal counsel, as long as the institution does not proceed through counsel. Students who have concurrent criminal charges pending against them, however, should be permitted to consult with counsel during their disciplinary hearings. The role of counsel may be limited to consultation (*Gabrilowitz*, 1978; see also *Henson*, 1983; *Moresco*, 1984).

13. Cases need not be dismissed on the ground that school officials failed to give students "Miranda" warnings about the right to remain silent. The Miranda rule has not been extended to the educational setting (*Boynton*, 1982).

14. A student subject to a serious penalty should be permitted to confront and cross-examine witnesses if the case will be decided on questions of credibility (*Winnick*, 1972). However, the institution is not required to devise a means to compel the attendance of witnesses (*Turof*, 1981), although it might be a good policy to do so.

15. Hearings in serious disciplinary cases should be tape recorded or transcribed. Furthermore, students who are found guilty of the charges against them should be given written reasons for such a determination (*Morale*, 1976).

16. Due process does not require that the decision of the hearing panel be unanimous. A simple majority vote would be sufficient (*Nzuve*, 1975).

17. A student who is found guilty of the charges should not be subject to an additional punishment simply for having pled innocent. However, a hearing panel may consider a pattern of lying and fabrication by the student at a hearing and may impose

a more severe penalty as a result (*United States*, 1978). Likewise, a student who is found guilty of the charges and who refuses to identify other participants in the misbehavior could be subject to an added punishment (*Roberts*, 1980).

18. In the absence of some sort of arbitrary discrimination, a decision to impose differing punishments in similar cases will be upheld if "reasonably and fairly made" (*Jones*, 1968, p. 203). Likewise, as in the larger society, it is not necessary to apprehend every wrongdoer before prosecuting those who have been caught (*Zanders*, 1968).

19. A just punishment imposed for reasons of deterrence is not incompatible with the educational mission of a school or college (*Petrey*, 1981; *Napolitano*, 1982).

20. Colleges and universities may establish disciplinary panels which make recommendations to an administrative officer who would review the record and the findings before making a final determination. Such a procedure may permit the administrative officer to correct any prior procedural errors (*Blanton*, 1973). Due process, however, does not require a formal right of appeal (*Reetz*, 1903; *National Union of Marine Cooks*, 1954; *Winnick*, 1972; Kaplin, 1978, p. 241).

21. Finally, the courts will expect both state and private institutions to follow their own regulations (*Tedeschi*, 1980; *Clayton*, 1981). Occasional harmless errors may be permitted, but campus officials will have to show that the deviations did not deny students a fair hearing (*Winnick, 1972; Turof*, 1981). Students may, of course, knowingly and freely waive a campus procedural requirement (*Yench*, 1973).

DISCIPLINE AS MORAL DEVELOPMENT

Proceduralism in student disciplinary proceedings can be remedied by appropriate revisions in school regulations. A more pernicious problem is the attitude of those campus administrators who regard the imposition of discipline as an unproductive exercise which should be supplanted by therapeutic alternatives. Unfortunately, administrators who adhere to such a perspective tend to overemphasize alternatives to discipline (such as "medical," psychiatric or psychological withdrawals), without ever understanding the underlying rationale for the disciplinary process, or its importance to individual students and the campus as a whole.

Perhaps the greatest benefit associated with the imposition of discipline on campus is that the language used to define prohibited conduct can also be relied upon to affirm a shared set of behavioral standards. One critical difference, for example, between a disciplinary suspension and a psychiatric withdrawal is that the latter is based upon hidden (or unknown) value judgments disguised by medical language. It is tempting to resort to such withdrawals frequently, in order to avoid the demanding task of articulating the ethical precepts which support the behavioral expectations of the community, or at least of the institution's administration. As a consequence, both the withdrawn student and the campus as a whole are left without any moral guidance.

The moral guidance offered by educators in a code of student conduct may be perceived as wrong, but articulating and enforcing moral values which others perceive as wrong at least encourages ethical thinking. It is reasonable to suggest in this regard that we have an "aimless" generation of young people (Yankelovich, 1981, p. xvi) partly because we have had a timid generation of educators, who have lacked the courage to confront students about the ethical dimensions of their behavior (Pavela, 1983).

One reason for the absence of ethical confrontation on campus has been the uncritical acceptance of the concept of moral relativism by many university administrators and faculty members. This attitude has led to a paralysis of some campus disciplinary systems, especially those with large and diverse student populations. Moral relativism is certainly not a new attitude in the American academic community, but its popularity dissipated after the Holocaust. That horrific event encouraged at least a temporary return to a Jeffersonian perspective that certain "self evident" truths and ethical values were applicable to "all men" and could be formulated in documents such as the United Nations *Universal Declaration of Human Rights*. Unfortunately, moral relativism may now be regaining some popularity; if so, it will be a popularity based on a profound ignorance of recent history.

It does require courage to affirm that campus disciplinary rules can be grounded in a code of moral conduct which should be applicable to all members of a diverse community. Kenneth Kenniston has observed in this regard that:

[t]here are many kinds of courage; needed here is the courage to risk being wrong, to risk doing unintentional harm and, above all, the courage to overcome one's own humility and sense of finite inadequacy. This is not merely diffuse 'courage to be' . . . but the resolve to be for something despite the perishability and transience of all human endeavors (Kenniston, 1971, p. 56).

The type of courage described by Kenniston does not require the stubborn and unreasoning adherence to an arbitrary set of standards. A moral commitment can be regarded as "hypothetical" and might be judged by its "actual consequences" in promoting the development of individuals and communities (Dewey, 1920, pp. 164-165; Geiger, 1947, pp. 157-193; Perry, 1981, p. 79). Accordingly, it is possible to remain open to new perspectives, while affirming a belief that there are certain "cardinal virtues" which "correspond to an experience so long and so nearly universal . . . [that] they seem to contain a deposited wisdom" of the human race (Lippmann, 1929, p. 226). Unfortunately, instead of encountering disciplinarians and counselors willing to make even a tentative commitment in this regard, the therapeutic approach presents students with a "placid, undifferentiated sympathy" which "discourage(s) precisely the kind of doubt, questioning and reflection" necessary to promote moral development (Simon, 1978, p. 135; see Hoffman, 1979).

Campus officials will also need courage to act on the realization that effective discipline requires just punishment. Such punishment is, and should be, unpleasant. The infliction of suffering is not an end in itself, however. Instead, as expressed by Thomas á Kempis over 500 years ago, "it is good that we sometimes have griefs and adversities, for they drive a man to behold himself" (1925, p. 22). Not surprisingly, it is when we "behold ourselves" in the context of a just punishment that we may be most receptive to ethical instruction.

The belief that a just punishment can promote the moral development of an offender is implicit in the concept of retribution. Essentially, retributive punishment affirms that there is a difference between right and wrong; that certain basic standards of moral behavior can be codified and enforced by the community; and that those who violate such standards should be held accountable for their behavior. These views were best expressed by Herbert Morris in a prize winning essay appearing in the *American Philosophical Quarterly*:

[m]y point is that law plays an indispensable role in our knowing what for society is good and evil. Failure to punish serious wrongdoing . . . would only serve to baffle our moral understanding. . . .

Further . . . punishment, among other things, permits purgation of guilt and ideally restoration of damaged relationships. Punishment, then, communicates what is wrong and in being imposed both rights the wrong and serves, as well, as a reminder of the evil done to others and to oneself in the doing of what is wrong. . . .

[Finally], the guilty wrongdoer is not viewed as damned by his wrongful conduct to a life forever divorced from others. He is viewed as a responsible being, responsible for having done wrong and possessing the capacity for recognizing the wrongfulness of his conduct (1981, p. 268).

The affirmation of personal responsibility implicit in retributive punishment is a critically important component of "personhood."* This is so because the imposition of a just punishment not only affirms that individuals are responsible for the bad things they do, but that they are also capable of making a moral choice to engage in good and constructive behavior. Naturally, the benefits associated with such an acceptance of responsibility are denied to students withdrawn on

---

*Perhaps the best expression of this perspective was set forth by Plato in the dialogue *Gorgias*. The dialogue is an excellent reading to incorporate in a training program for members of the campus judiciary.

medical grounds. Indeed, under the pretense of devising a humane procedure, campus administrators may actually dehumanize those students by asserting that they lack the capacity to be held accountable for their actions. This concept was well expressed by Antoine de Saint-Exupery in *Flight to Arras* (1942): "[i]f, intending to absolve myself, I plead fate as the excuse for my misfortunes, I subject myself to fate. But, if I accept responsibility, I affirm my strength as a man. I am able to influence that of which I am a part. I declare myself a constituent part of the community of mankind" (p. 417).

It is important to affirm that almost all human beings have at least some freedom to make rational choices, in order to avoid engendering feelings of helplessness and dependency. Recent studies have shown that individuals "who have a sense of some responsibility for a crisis may also have a feeling of control. Helplessness, it seems, is one of the most destructive of all feelings. . . ." (Brody, 1984, p. c1). Christopher Lasch summarized this position when he wrote that "a genuine affirmation of the self . . . insists on a core of selfhood not subject to environmental determination, even under extreme conditions" (Lasch, 1984, p. 39).

Finally, one frequently overlooked attribute of the disciplinary process is that students who are accused of disciplinary violations may be able to engage in substantive discussions with decision-makers about the underlying wisdom or fairness of a university regulation. Students withdrawn on psychiatric grounds are not usually accorded such an opportunity, since psychiatric diagnosis "locates the source of aberration within the individual" (Rosenhan, 1973, p. 253) and encourages administrators to focus exclusively on student "pathology." Likewise, students subject to disciplinary sanctions can compare the nature of the infraction for which they were held responsible with the punishment which was imposed. It is therefore possible to make an appeal to justice or fairness in seeking to modify the result. Students withdrawn on psychiatric grounds, however, are told that the action is taken to "help" them and to insure that they obtain longer term "therapy." Appeals to justice appear to make no sense in such a "medical" context, even though the result may be comparable to a disciplinary suspension or expulsion.

MORAL DEVELOPMENT AND HUMANISTIC VALUES

The concept of using a campus disciplinary system to promote moral growth will concern some observers, who fear that such an effort reflects a return to the behavioral standards imposed upon students in the 1950s. This is a dangerous misconception which has the potential to undermine support for the disciplinary process and to induce even greater reliance upon mandatory psychiatric or psychological withdrawals. Those who see a legitimate connection between student discipline and moral development will need to make a convincing argument that the imposition of discipline at a secular institution can be grounded upon humanistic values which are fully compatible with a modern pluralistic society.

In 1929, during a period when traditional values were questioned throughout the Western world, one commentator made an observation which is equally applicable in the aftermath of the cultural transformations of the 1960s and 1970s. In *A Preface to Morals*, Walter Lippmann wrote that "[m]orality has become so stereotyped, so thin and verbal, so encrusted with pious fraud . . . that our generation has almost forgotten that virtue was not invented in Sunday schools but derives originally from a profound realization of the character of human life" (p. 227). This was a perspective shared nearly fifty years later, and applied to the modern American university, when Edward D. Eddy concluded that most institutions of higher education "have given up moralism without having any compelling morality to offer in its place" (1977, p. 8).

One of the last remaining ways in which the university offers any explicit moral guidance is in the dissemination of a code of student conduct. Fortunately, having learned from excesses in the past, most institutions no longer seek to regulate the private, consensual sexual behavior of students, require participation in religious activities, set a standard of dress or appearance, or prohibit the lawful expression of unpopular social and political views. The days when students would be subject to disciplinary action for failing to attend religious services at a state university (*North*, 1891), or because they publicly criticized the campus administration (*Steier*, 1959), or simply because they were "apparently not in sympathy with the management of the institution" (*Woods*, 1924, p. 550) are over. Instead, the typical code of conduct found at most colleges and universities is restricted to defining and protecting the minimal, essential requirements for group living and personal safety. Those who suggest that the strict enforcement of such regulations reflects a "return to the standards of the 1950s" may lack a clear and accurate impression of the 1950s.

Limiting the scope of a campus disciplinary code gives each student at least some latitude to develop a broader and more comprehensive definition of virtue. Such a result is desirable, since it promotes the continuing evolution and refinement of moral perspectives. Moreover, the equitable enforcement of basic behavioral standards is usually regarded by most members of the campus community as a reasonable exercise of institutional authority. Under these circumstances, it is much easier to engage students in ethical dialogue.*

---

*See "Baxter and His History Professor" in Appendix II, p. 75.

For example, at the University of Maryland, students involved in "disciplinary conferences" are often encouraged to reflect upon the code of ethical behavior set forth by Confucius nearly 2,500 years ago: "[w]hat you do not like when done to yourself do not do to others" (Singer, 1967, p. 365). Building upon that foundation, one may then discuss the likelihood that there are certain affirmative ethical responsibilities incumbent upon human beings; for example, as expressed by Antoine de Saint Exupery; "[t]o be a man is, precisely, to be responsible . . . [i]t is to feel, when setting one's stone, that one is contributing to the building of the world." (1942, p. 37). Finally, the campus environment and the nature of scholarship itself provide a means to affirm a number of specific virtues, including the willingness "to listen honestly and tolerantly to evidence from whatever source, to entertain alternative points of view with respect, to engage in self-judgment and self-criticism, and to abandon results that gratify the ego but simply aren't true" (Eddy, 1977, p. 14). Naturally, the potential benefits of these discussions would be lost if educators were primarily concerned with ritualistic adherence to courtroom procedures, or if students accused of misconduct were readily withdrawn on "medical" grounds.

Ethical dialogue in the disciplinary setting has a significant and rightful place in the secular university. This is so because effective dialogue promotes intellectual honesty and candor, encourages the participants to treat each other with courtesy, and fosters intellectual inquiry. In the broadest sense, such a process is likely to lead to an affirmation of two fundamental, humanistic values: respect for individual freedom, and an obligation to make a constructive contribution to community life.

Individual freedom is occasionally confused with license. However, upon reflection, most individuals appreciate that genuine freedom is premised upon order and self discipline, not the unrestrained satisfaction of every whim or impulse. The latter can be compared to a municipality without traffic regulations. When motorists are "free" to do exactly as they please, the end result is confusion, mayhem, and less mobility for everyone.

Likewise, the conception of individual freedom in the American social and political tradition has been premised upon the acceptance of responsibility. Freedom from the arbitrary and unreasonable standards set by others did not mean freedom from any standards at all. As exemplified by the program for personal moral development in Benjamin Franklin's *Autobiography*, the standards set by the free individual could be even more demanding than those established by the state or church. Indeed, one need not share Franklin's objective of reaching "moral perfection" (see Wolf, 1982) to appreciate that his example reveals the essence of what should be taught about individual freedom: namely, that the fullest exercise of freedom consists of the deliberate pursuit of personal moral growth;* and that moral growth entails the development of reason and conscience in order to restrain and choose among the endless series of appetites and desires which entice all human beings.

A second fundamental value which can be affirmed in the secular university is the moral obligation to make some constructive contribution to the life of the community. Our very survival and evolution as a species has depended upon "sophisticated cooperative behavior" (Wilson, 1978, p. 138; see Niebuhr, 1965, p. 112). The human capacity to engage in such behavior has created the social and political mechanisms which can permit the free individual to grow and flourish. In this sense, it seems appropriate to suggest that the enforcement of reasonable community values not only protects the community, but promotes the personal development of each individual within the community. The latter consideration, in the educational setting, seemed especially important to Justice Lewis Powell, who wrote that:

[e]ducation in any meaningful sense includes the inculcation of an understanding in each pupil of the necessity of rules and obedience thereto. This understanding is no less important than learning to read and write. One who does not comprehend the meaning and necessity of discipline is handicapped not merely in his education but throughout his subsequent life. In an age when the home and church play a diminishing role in shaping the character and value judgments of the young, a heavier responsibility falls upon the schools. When an immature student merits censure for his conduct, he is rendered a disservice if appropriate sanctions are not applied . . . (dissenting in Goss, 1975, p. 593).

Individuals are able to develop and mature within communities because community life can be both nurturing and challenging. For example, in the university environment, we endeavor to protect students from arbitrary decision-making, but we also challenge them to adhere to a fair, but strict, standard of personal conduct. Such a challenge will occasionally result in conflict or controversy. However, instead of fearing conflict, we appreciate that "individuals who attain high levels of complexity in feeling, thinking, and judging do so as a result of conflict, not its absence" (Kenniston, 1971, p. 388).

In short, educators should concern themselves with student moral development. Such development can be enhanced through the disciplinary process. The values affirmed through the disciplinary process

---

*This perspective is not incompatible with traditional religious teachings. For example, Aleksandr Solzhenitsyn has observed that:

[s]ince his body is doomed to death, [man's] task on earth evidently must be more spiritual: not a total engrossment in everyday life, not the search for the best ways to obtain material goods and then their carefree consumption. It has to be the fulfillment of a permanent earnest duty so that one's life journey may become above all an experience of moral growth: to leave life a better human being than one started it (1980, p. 19).

include a respect for individual freedom and the obligation to make a constructive contribution to the life of the community. The end result of these efforts may be the finest product of the educational enterprise: free, mature, and responsible human beings.

SUMMARY

The focus of inquiry in any psychological or psychiatric withdrawal procedure must be on specific, usually prohibited, behavior which indicates that the student poses a physical threat to self or to others, or is otherwise unable to meet reasonable institutional standards. With very few exceptions, these are precisely the forms of behavior which college and university disciplinary systems should be designed to address. Some administrators are inclined to avoid the disciplinary process in serious cases, since campus disciplinary procedures may be too cumbersome and legalistic. This problem should be resolved by carefully reviewing pertinent court decisions and developing less formal and adversarial disciplinary policies. Another reason why administrators readily rely on mandatory withdrawal policies is because they do not understand the underlying rationale for the disciplinary process. The imposition of discipline is important to individual students, and to the campus as a whole, because it affirms a shared set of behavioral standards, encourages ethical thinking and dialogue, and teaches students that they are responsible for their actions.

Chapter VI

Appropriate Uses of a Mandatory Withdrawal Policy

There may be rare occasions when resort to a mandatory withdrawal policy might be necessary, especially at those schools where administrators are reluctant to rely exclusively on state involuntary commitment procedures. For example, students suffering from a mental disorder who commit disciplinary offenses without knowing the nature or the wrongfulness of their actions might be candidates for mandatory withdrawal. Also, students who attempt to commit suicide, and who are likely to do so again, might properly be withdrawn. In any event, a mandatory withdrawal in most circumstances would not be sufficient. Campus officials, in cooperation with a student's parents, if possible, should attempt to arrange for prompt referral to an appropriate facility for observation, evaluation, and treatment.

DIVERTING STUDENTS FROM THE DISCIPLINARY PROCESS

A student suffering from a mental disorder who did not violate the institution's reasonable standards of conduct might be offered some form of counseling or therapy, but should not be withdrawn from school on psychiatric grounds. Even though the student might be dismissed for academic deficiencies, the stigma associated with an academic dismissal is far less damaging than that which would result from a mandatory psychiatric or psychological withdrawal. This is so, in the words of a past president of the National Association for Mental Health, because those individuals referred for psychiatric evaluation or treatment "are still being subjected to the unfounded fears of people around them" (Chase, 1972, p. 85; see also *Lombard*, 1975; *Sawyer*, 1978). Those fears can have a lifelong impact, as demonstrated by the pubic reaction to the disclosure during the 1972 presidential campaign that Senator Thomas Eagleton had undergone psychiatric treatment approximately ten years earlier.

The practical problem on most campuses, however, is not the passive student in need of psychiatric treatment. Instead, what seems to be of most concern to administrators are students who are apparently suffering from a mental disorder, and who engage in behavior which significantly disrupts the academic process, or which threatens their physical safety, or the safety of others.

As suggested in the preceding section, colleges and universities should depend upon a properly drafted disciplinary code in order to protect the campus community. Such a code would vest campus administrators with sufficient authority to suspend or expel students who persistently or substantially disrupt the academic process, or who physically harm (or threaten to harm) others. It must be emphasized, however, that students perceived as eccentric should not be dismissed from school simply because their presence might be considered disturbing to "conventional" students. Indeed, educators should understand that students gain a sense of perspective and have opportunities for a "wider . . . range of satisfying relationships" if they learn some reasonable tolerance for the "idiosyncratic deviances" of others (Chickering, 1969, p. 97).

Even if a student did violate campus disciplinary regulations, there may be cases in which it would be unjust to impose disciplinary sanctions. For example, a student who was suffering from a mental disorder and, as a result of that mental disorder, thought he was squeezing lemons while he choked his roommate should not be held fully accountable for his actions. Instead, campus officials might rely upon a mandatory withdrawal policy rather than a disciplinary suspension or expulsion in order to remove the student from campus.

Any decision to rely upon a mandatory withdrawal policy in lieu of disciplinary action should be guided by some articulated standard. Given the various benefits associated with the imposition of discipline, such a standard should be very narrowly defined. Essentially, a student suffering from a mental disorder who is accused of a disciplinary violation should not be diverted from the disciplinary process unless the student, as the result of the mental disorder: (a) lacks the capacity to respond to the charges or (b) did not know the nature or wrongfulness of the conduct at the time of the offense.

Some psychiatrists and psychologists may oppose any standard for mandatory withdrawals which emphasizes cognitive dysfunction rather than affective or "emotional" impairment. Nonetheless, substantial numbers of mental health professionals are now endorsing equally strict formulations for use in the courts. For example, three prominent psychiatrists recently observed in the *Psychiatric Annals* that "the question of whether persons with disturbances of volition and/or behavior, such as personality disorders, impulse disorders, substance use disorders and psychosexual disorders ought to be held accountable for their illegal acts we readily answer in the affirmative" (Rachlin, Holpern, Portnow, 1984, p. 147). This point of view is also reflected in a 1983 American Psychiatric Association policy statement, which approved limiting the insanity defense in criminal cases to "only those severely abnormal mental conditions that grossly and demonstrably impair a person's perception or understanding of reality . . ." (*Third Branch*, 1983, p. 2).

One reason why increasing numbers of mental health professionals are inclined to limit any claim of mental illness as an exculpatory defense is an awareness that "it dignifies rather than debases the mentally ill to hold them responsible" for most of their actions (N. Morris, 1983, p. 146). Indeed, a number of respected observers and organizations, including the American Medical Association, would abolish the insanity defense altogether (*Washington Post*, Dec. 7, 1983, p. A4), largely on the ground that it is "therapeutically desirable to treat behavioral deviants as responsible for their conduct rather than as involuntary victims playing a sick role" (Robinson, 1970, p. 251). These perspectives are rooted in an outpouring of recent scholarly literature defending the concept that nearly all human beings have at least some capacity to make moral choices (see, generally, Eccles and Robinson, 1984; Moore, 1984; Samenow, 1984; Gaylin, 1982; Menninger, 1973).

Unfortunately, the concept of moral accountability is anathema to those educators who view any disciplinary infraction as evidence of underlying mental or emotional "illness." Campus officials who share that point of view are then inclined to see the most serious disciplinary violations as almost certain evidence that the accused student must be suffering from a profound mental disorder, thereby requiring medical or psychiatric removal from the institution. At heart, this perspective is premised upon a basic distrust of the concept of freedom of choice, and reflects a misunderstanding which has been effectively challenged by Erich Fromm (1964):

[t]he argument for the view that man has no freedom to choose the better as against the worse is to some considerable extent based on the fact that one looks usually at the last decision in a chain of events, and not at the first or the second ones. Indeed, at the point of final decision the freedom to choose has usually vanished. But it may still have been there at an earlier point when the person was not yet deeply caught in his own passions. One might generalize by saying that one of the reasons why most people fail in their lives is precisely because they are not aware of the point when they are still free to act according to reason. . . (p. 135).

In short, it is likely that the vast majority of students accused of violating institutional regulations can and should be held accountable for their behavior. Although psychiatric labeling and mandatory withdrawals may be perceived as more humane in the short run, both of those practices dehumanize students by creating the impression that they are incapable of making moral choices. The proper use for a mandatory withdrawal policy would be in the extraordinary case of a student who violated significant institutional regulations, was suffering from a mental disorder which produced a grossly distorted impression of reality, and who could not be withdrawn and referred for treatment on a voluntary basis.

RESPONDING TO SUICIDAL STUDENTS

A second possible use for a mandatory psychiatric withdrawal policy might be to remove suicidal students from campus. It would be unwise, however, to adopt a policy which required the automatic removal of all students who threatened to harm themselves. This is so, in part, because suicidal persons are "not necessarily mentally ill" (Schneidman and Mandelkorn, 1970, p. 130; see also Wolfe and Cotler, 1973, p. 310). Furthermore, suicidal behavior does not always indicate that a student is unable to cope with academic stress (Bernard and Bernard, 1980). For example, a recent survey by *Newsweek* magazine suggested that considerations such as "uncertainty about the future," "financial worries," and "loneliness," might also be important factors in student suicide on campus (*Newsweek on Campus*, December 1983, p. 26).

While it cannot be disputed that many suicidal students are concerned about academic competition, there are other important causes for suicide which need to be considered, usually in conjunction with student apprehension about grades. For example, one scholar has found that social isolation was a "major precipitating factor" in student suicides (Seiden, 1966, p. 399; see also Wolfe and Cotler, 1973, p. 306; see generally Alvarez, 1973, pp. 91-92). Others have concluded that a correlation appears to exist in many suicidal students between the "past or present loss of an intimate person" and "concerns about studying effectively" (Blaine and Carmen, 1968, p. 837; see also Seiden, 1971, pp. 246-247). Feelings associated with a sense of loss and social isolation may also explain why some studies indicate that there is an "over-representation of freshmen" among the undergraduates who attempt suicide (Wolfe and Cotler, 1973, p. 310).

Essentially, college and university officials can and should do more to create an atmosphere in which suicidal behavior is less likely, rather than simply withdrawing students who threaten or attempt to commit suicide (Bernard and Bernard, 1982). Striving to develop more of a sense of community on campus would be important, along with a willingness to define and enforce high standards of personal behavior. The latter might seem anomalous, unless one makes a comparison with family life and the suicidal behavior of children. In this regard, Dr.

Michael Peck, consultant to the Los Angeles Suicide Prevention Center, has observed that:

> a close, involved, loving family is the overall best suicide prevention factor. A lot of parents are afraid of their children, afraid to set rules and enforce them. A feeling that they can do anything they want is terrifying to kids. They fear a loss of control (1984, p. 8E).

Dr. Peck's views may be pertinent to the campus environment, because a number of studies have indicated that increasing numbers of young Americans "lack clearly defined goals and feel utterly aimless about their lives" (Yankelovich, 1981, p. xvi; see also Levine, 1980, p. 21). As a result, "scores of young people" interviewed by one writer complained about the absence of proper discipline and "the lack of challenging responsibilities against which they could shape their character" (Morgan, 1981, p. A16; see also, Lasch, 1979, p. 308). If these observations are correct, a strict, but fair code of conduct on campus may contribute to an environment in which students are encouraged to acquire a critically important sense of moral direction and purpose.

The availability of counseling services and other forms of support for students should also be a part of an effective suicide prevention program. Many individuals who attempt suicide "had experienced a progressive isolation from meaningful social relationships" and lacked someone "to tell [their] troubles to" (Topal and Reznikoff, 1982, pp. 142, 148). A first step in addressing that problem could be the development of a "close and significant relationship with a guidance counselor" (Seiden, 1971, p. 247). It would seem reasonable for colleges and universities to provide such counseling, rather than routinely withdrawing suicidal students on psychiatric grounds. The latter approach, by returning students to what may be a destructive family environment, could further isolate them from their peers, "thus intensifying rather than alleviating their distress" (Bernard and Bernard, 1980, p. 111). This potential outcome is all the more regrettable since, in many cases, "even the most suicidal person is a danger to himself only a relatively brief period of time, perhaps a . . . few days out of a total life span of many years" (Seiden, 1971, p. 248).

There does remain one conceivable circumstance in which the mandatory withdrawal of a suicidal student would be appropriate. Basically, it might not be feasible to render ongoing assistance to a student who had engaged in self-destructive behavior and who was suffering from a serious mental disorder which was being exacerbated in the academic environment. This is not unlike the situation encountered by New York University in the *Doe* (1981) case, when a self-destructive medical student with a serious, "recognized [mental] disorder" which would require "long-term treatment" encountered the "exceptional stresses" of medical education (*Doe*, 1981, pp. 778-779,

Notes 9 and 10). There may be no alternative under these circumstances but to initiate mandatory withdrawal proceedings, especially since it would not seem just to subject the individual to the moral condemnation associated with disciplinary action.

If a suicidal student is withdrawn from school for psychiatric reasons, it will be imperative to make some reasonable effort to refer the student for psychiatric care. This is important, since some individuals who engage in suicidal behavior will need prompt hospitalization (Litman, 1970, p. 408). Ironically, those campus officials who would be quick to withdraw a student on the ground that the institution might otherwise be liable for preventing the student's suicide should understand that their legal risks are substantially greater if they simply "dump" suicidal students in the larger community. Such a practice is embarrassingly similar to the "obligatory departures" of insane people from medieval European towns (Foucault, 1973, p. 8), and is ethically indefensible.

STUDENTS WITH EATING DISORDERS

There may also be rare occasions when students suffering from certain eating disorders should be withdrawn on medical grounds. The most likely candidates for withdrawal would be students in serious medical jeopardy, who could not receive effective treatment on campus, or whose condition was made worse in a campus setting. This would be a circumstance not unlike that of a suicidal student suffering from a serious mental disorder which was being exacerbated in the academic environment. However, as in the general category of suicidal behavior, it would not be prudent to adopt a policy requiring the automatic removal of all students suffering from any eating disorder.

The two eating disorders of most immediate concern to college and university officials are anorexia nervosa and bulimia. The former is identified by "intense fear of becoming obese, disturbance of body image, significant weight loss, refusal to maintain a minimal normal body weight" and absence of menstrual periods (*Diagnostic and Statistical Manual or Mental Disorders*, 1980, pp. 67, 69). The latter is associated with binge eating, usually followed by purging or vomiting. Some characteristics of both disorders can be combined in individuals whom some mental health professionals would label as "bulimarexic" (Brenner, 1980, p. 58). It has been estimated that nearly five percent of all young women suffer from anorexia; about 15 percent from bulimia (*U.S. News and World Report*, Oct. 8, 1984, p. 62).

The causes of anorexia and bulimia appear to be extraordinarily complex. There is a growing consensus that many individuals suffering from those disorders have been subject to intense family pressures to achieve and excel (Bemis, 1978, pp. 596, 601). Anorexics and bulimics are often perfectionists who set unreasonable standards for themselves (Brenner, 1980, p. 1; Bemis, 1978, p. 595) and who normally have low self esteem (Enright and Sansone, 1983, p. 1). Loneliness, feelings of rejection, a "struggle for . . . self respect" and an intense fear of "disapproval and rejection" are also common characteristics (*Anred Alert*, 1983, pp. 1-2). These psychological factors may be influenced by physiological or bio-chemical attributes, including "an immature pattern of hypothalamic functioning" in anorexics (Lucas, 1978, p. 1), or a variety of clinical depression in some anorexics and bulimics (*Mental Health Update*, 1984, p. 2). What is beyond dispute is that most students with eating disorders have also been affected by social pressures which suggest that self-worth can be defined by body weight. One of the best examples of such social pressure is a frequently recurring health spa advertisement in the *New York Times*, in which an attractive young woman is pictured next to the following statement:

[s]he's in heavenly shape. Wherever she turns, the world responds to her beautifully. Be it physically, mentally, professionally or socially, she's in control. A lady who keeps her energy in orbit by keeping her body in shape . . . Shape your world too. . . (*New York Times*, Oct. 1, 1984, p. A12).

The various psychological, medical, and social causes of anorexia and bulimia are reflected in the variety of treatments developed by mental health professionals. Individual psychotherapy, group therapy, family therapy, behavioral conditioning, and the use of anti-depressant drugs have been recommended for different clients or patients in different settings. In any event, for whatever reason, it has been determined "that approximately two-thirds of anorexic patients recover or improve, with one third remaining chronically ill or dying of the disorder" (Bemis, 1978, p. 597). A comparable or higher rate of success may be encountered in bulimics, along with lower mortality rates.

A few basic suggestions about the treatment of eating disorders appear to be supported by many knowledgeable observers (see generally, Lucas, 1978, 1981; Brenner, 1980; *Anred Alert*, 1983; *Mental Health Update*, 1984; Rigotti, 1984):

1. Preventive efforts may be used to discourage some susceptible individuals from developing eating disorders. For example, mental health professionals might conduct relevant seminars or information sessions for appropriate groups on campus, such as sororities and social clubs.

2. Those students who appear to be suffering from an eating disorder should be given a thorough physical examination, including analysis of electrolyte balance and hydration. Medical treatment for malnutrition may be necessary. It is important to understand in this regard that any eccentric behavior by the

student may be due to the symptoms of starvation, rather than any underlying mental disorder.

3. A direct and candid discussion of the disorder might be undertaken, with emphasis upon the social and psychological pressures contributing to it. Basic nutritional information should also be provided. A program of medically approved exercise might also be considered, in order to avoid osteoporosis (a brittle bone disease).

4. Realistic goals for proper nutrition should be initiated, along with a carefully monitored, step-by-step program to reach those goals. Food logs and meal plans might be useful.

5. Appropriate therapy should be offered for any underlying mental disorder. Counseling efforts should focus, in part, on improving self image and self esteem. Family involvement may be desirable and would not be precluded by the Buckley Amendment if the student is a financial dependent or if an "emergency" exists.

6. Unresponsive patients with potentially life threatening complications should be committed to a medical facility for prompt intervention, as necessary.

The foregoing analysis suggests that most students suffering from eating disorders could remain in a campus environment, provided that some reasonable support services were available. Indeed, as in the case of certain suicidal students, it might be harmful to routinely withdraw a student with an eating disorder, since many such students are "inordinately sensitive to rejection" (Brenner, 1980, p. 59) and could be placed in greater jeopardy as a result.

Based upon advice specifically solicited for this monograph, a number of nationally recognized authorities on eating disorders have suggested the following:

1. There will be cases in which it would actually be helpful for the anorexic or bulimic to remain on campus, separated from the home environment, "where the eating disorder behaviors may have been rooted," provided that "appropriate treatment services are available." In this regard, it would be ideal if colleges and universities "had on staff, a professional trained in treatment of anorexia and bulimia" (Melick, 1983, p. 1).

2. Generally, "if the anorexia is caught early, and if treatment is begun and is proceeding in a positive direction, it would seem counterproductive to remove the student from college." Such a practice might "exacerbate the sense of isolation and only encourage further withdrawal from life situations and friends" (Rubel, 1983, p. 1).

3. Many anorexics and bulimics "are able to function adequately," even in "extremely difficult" academic programs, including engineering (Halvorson, 1983, p. 1).

4. However, there may be instances in which "adjustment to college life . . . can increase the eating disordered individual's stress level in such a way as to further the eating disorder" (Melick, 1983, p. 1). Likewise, "a seriously emaciated anorexic who is obviously in medical jeopardy and a state of mental and emotional confusion is an appropriate candidate for hospitalization and probably should not return to college until, through therapy, she has established more . . . effective coping mechanisms" (Rubel, 1983, p. 1).

Once again, as in the case of suicidal behavior, the response to students with eating disorders will have to take into consideration the special facts and circumstances of each case. Broadly written withdrawal policies, used routinely and automatically, may do more harm than good. Reasonable and relatively uncomplicated treatment programs can be offered by most college and university counseling or health centers, thereby permitting the majority of students with eating disorders to continue their studies.

SUMMARY

The use of mandatory psychiatric or psychological withdrawals should be avoided whenever possible, since the stigma associated with a finding of some sort of mental or emotional disorder can be very damaging. Basically, students who are merely eccentric or who simply "cause concern" to others should not be subject to mandatory withdrawal. Furthermore, if a student has violated institutional disciplinary regulations, a mandatory withdrawal should be initiated only if the student lacks the capacity to respond to the disciplinary charges, or did not know the nature and wrongfulness of the act in question. Also, in instances of threatened or attempted suicide, it is recommended that students be subject to mandatory withdrawal only if they are suffering from a serious mental disorder which is being exacerbated in the campus environment. Finally, students suffering from eating disorders should be withdrawn only if their condition is made worse in the academic setting, or if they are in serious medical jeopardy and cannot receive effective treatment without leaving the college or university.

Chapter VII

Conclusions

It would not be administratively sound or legally sufficient to use vague and ambiguous labels (e.g., "disturbed," "behavior of concern to others," "abnormal") to remove a student from a college or university. Instead, if "medical" language must be used, it is best to use words capable of at least some professionally accepted meaning, such as the term "mental disorder," used in the current American Psychiatric Association Diagnostic Manual. Furthermore, good administrative practice and (at public institutions) current constitutional standards, require some minimal due process protections before students can be removed on psychiatric grounds. Removal on the basis of a mental disorder alone, however, would be precluded by Section 504 of the Rehabilitation Act of 1973, even with sufficient procedural due process. Consequently, the focus of inquiry must be upon specific, usually prohibited, behavior. It is recommended, on policy grounds, to rely upon the disciplinary process in response to incidents of such prohibited behavior, unless the student lacks the capacity to respond to the charges, or did not know the nature or wrongfulness of the act in question. Furthermore, in cases of threatened or attempted suicide, or in cases in which students are suffering from eating disorders, an initial effort should be made to allow the affected student to remain on campus. If the student is to be withdrawn, school officials should refer the student to an appropriate facility for professional observation and evaluation.

Appendix I

Standards and Procedures for Involuntary Administrative Withdrawal[1]

STANDARDS FOR WITHDRAWAL

1. A student will be subject to involuntary administrative withdrawal from the University, or from University housing, if it is determined, by clear and convincing evidence, that the student is suffering from a mental disorder,[2] and, as a result of the mental disorder:

   (a) engages, or threatens to engage, in behavior which poses a danger of causing physical harm to self or others, or

   (b) engages, or threatens to engage, in behavior which would cause significant property damage, or directly and substantially impede the lawful activities of others.

2. These standards do not preclude removal from the University, or University housing, in accordance with provisions of the residence hall occupancy agreement, or other University rules or regulations.

VIOLATIONS OF DISCIPLINARY REGULATIONS

3. A student accused of violating University disciplinary regulations may be diverted from the disciplinary process and withdrawn in accordance with these standards, if the student, as a result of mental disorder:

   (a) lacks the capacity to respond to pending disciplinary charges, or

---

[1]These proposed standards and procedures are designed to stimulate discussion and analysis. It will be important to confer with counsel for your institution in order to design an appropriate policy. Also, some institutions may not resort to mandatory psychological or psychiatric withdrawals under any circumstances.

[2]It would be advisable to rely upon the definitions for various mental disorders provided by the current *American Psychiatric Association Diagnostic Manual* (DSM-III). See the discussion on pp. 24-25, *supra*.

(b) did not know the nature or wrongfulness of the conduct at the time of the offense.[3]

4. Students subject to disciplinary charges who wish to introduce relevant evidence of any mental disorder must so inform the Dean of Students[4] in writing at least two business days prior to any disciplinary hearing.[5] If the Dean determines that the evidence may have merit, the case shall then be resolved in accordance with these standards and procedures. Thereafter, if it is determined that the student does not meet the criteria set forth in part three, the case will be returned to the disciplinary process. Evidence of any mental disorder may not be admitted into evidence or considered by the hearing panel in any disciplinary proceeding.[6]

REFERRAL FOR EVALUATION

5. The Dean of Students may refer a student for evaluation by an independent licensed psychiatrist or psychologist chosen by the institution, if the Dean reasonably believes that the student may meet the criteria set forth in Part one, or if a student subject to disciplinary charges wishes to introduce relevant evidence of any mental disorder.

6. Students referred for evaluation in accordance with this Part shall be so informed in writing, either by personal delivery or by certified mail, and shall be given a copy of these standards and procedures. The evaluation must be completed within five business days from the date of the referral letter, unless an extension is granted by the Dean in writing. Students may be accompanied by a licensed psychologist or psychiatrist of their choice, who may observe, but

---

[3]Under the first clause of this standard, a student suffering from a mental disorder who thought he was squeezing lemons while he choked his roommate would be diverted from the disciplinary process. This is so because the student did not know the nature of the act in question. Likewise, under the second clause, the same result would be reached in the case of a psychotic student who attacked one of his teachers after receiving delusional directives from God. Although the student knew the nature of the act, he did not know the act was wrong. Finally, in a third example, a student with a reported "compulsion" to steal or set fires would not be excused from the disciplinary process, since the student would know the nature of the act, as well as its wrongfulness.

[4]The title may vary at different institutions.

[5]Such notice may also be given by a family member, or by others advising or assisting the student.

[6]This is a very strict standard which some schools may wish to modify. For example, it might be possible to permit consideration of a mental disorder as a mitigating factor in determining sanctions. However, the disadvantage of the latter approach is that complex and potentially misleading or inaccurate psychiatric testimony may be introduced into proceedings in which critical scrutiny of the testimony is unlikely. Perhaps the best approach would be to preclude the presentation of such testimony before a hearing panel, but to allow an administrative officer to review it before acting upon the panel's recommendation. The recommended penalty may then be reduced by the administrative officer, as appropriate.

not participate in the evaluation process. Legal representation will not be permitted.

7. Any pending disciplinary action may be withheld until the evaluation is completed, in the discretion of the Dean of Students.

8. A student who fails to complete the evaluation in accordance with these standards and procedures may be withdrawn on an interim basis, as set forth in Parts 9-12, or referred for disciplinary action, or both.

INTERIM WITHDRAWAL

9. An interim administrative withdrawal may be implemented immediately if a student fails to complete an evaluation, as provided by Parts five and six of these standards and procedures. Also, an interim withdrawal may be implemented immediately if the Dean of Students determines that a student may be suffering from a mental disorder, and the student's behavior poses an imminent danger of:

   (a) causing serious physical harm to the student or others, or,

   (b) causing significant property damage, or directly and substantially impeding the lawful activities of others.

10. A student subject to an interim withdrawal shall be given written notice of the withdrawal either by personal delivery or by certified mail, and shall be given a copy of these standards and procedures. The student shall then be given an opportunity to appear personally before the Dean of Students, or a designee, within two business days from the effective date of the interim withdrawal, in order to review the following issues only:

    (a) the reliability of the information concerning the student's behavior;

    (b) whether or not the student's behavior poses a danger of causing imminent, serious physical harm to the student or others, causing significant property damage, or directly and substantially impeding the lawful activities of others;

    (c) whether or not the student has completed an evaluation, in accordance with these standards and procedures.

11. A student subject to interim withdrawal may be assisted in the proceeding specified at Part 10 by a family member and a licensed psychologist or psychiatrist, or in lieu of a licensed psychologist or psychiatrist, by a member of the faculty or staff of the institution.[7] Furthermore, the student may be accompanied by legal counsel, although the role of counsel will be limited to providing

---

[7]In this part, and in Part 13(d), a university faculty or staff member who is an attorney will be regarded as "legal counsel."

legal advice to the student. Students will be expected to speak for themselves whenever possible.

12. An informal hearing, as provided in Part 13, will be held within seven business days after the student has been evaluated by the appropriate mental health professional. Such evaluation should be undertaken within two business days after the student submits a proper request for an appointment. The student will remain withdrawn on an interim basis pending completion of the informal hearing, but will be allowed to enter upon the campus to attend the hearing, or for other necessary purposes, as authorized in writing by the Dean of Students.

INFORMAL HEARING

13. Students subject to an involuntary withdrawal shall be accorded an informal hearing before the Dean of Students, or a designee. The following guidelines will be applicable:

    (a) Students will be informed of the time, date, and location of the informal hearing, in writing, either by personal delivery or certified mail, at least two business days in advance.

    (b) The entire case file, including an evaluation prepared pursuant to Part five of these standards and procedures, and the names of prospective witnesses, will be available for inspection by the student in the Dean of Student's office during normal business hours. The file, which should be available at least two business days before the informal hearing, need not include the personal and confidential notes of any institutional official or participant in the evaluation process.

    (c) The informal hearing shall be conversational and non-adversarial. Formal rules of evidence will not apply. The Dean or designee shall exercise active control over the proceedings to avoid needless consumption of time and to achieve the orderly completion of the hearing. Any person who disrupts the hearing may be excluded.

    (d) The student may choose to be assisted by a family member and a licensed psychologist or psychiatrist, or, in lieu of a licensed psychologist or psychiatrist, by a member of the faculty or staff of the institution. Furthermore, the student may be accompanied by legal counsel, although the role of counsel will be limited to providing legal advice to the student.

    (e) Those assisting the student, except for legal counsel, will be given reasonable time to ask relevant questions of any individual appearing at the informal hearing, as well as to present relevant evidence.

    (f) A tenured faculty member will be appointed to review and challenge any evaluation containing a recommendation for involuntary withdrawal. The faculty member will be selected in advance by the Chair of Faculty Senate [or other appropriate faculty body]. The faculty member shall be given notice of the informal hearing, and access to the case file, in accordance with sections (a) and (b) of this Part. Furthermore, the faculty member will be given reasonable time at the hearing to ask relevant questions and to present relevant evidence designed to challenge the involuntary withdrawal recommendation.

(g) Whenever possible, the student will be expected to respond to questions asked by the Dean or designee. Students who refuse to answer on grounds of the Fifth Amendment privilege may be informed that the Dean or designee could draw a negative inference from their refusal which might result in their dismissal from the institution, in accordance with these standards and procedures.[8]

(h) The informal hearing may be conducted in the absence of a student who fails to appear after proper notice.

(i) The mental health professional who prepared the evaluation pursuant to Part five of these standards and procedures may be expected to appear at the informal hearing, and to respond to relevant questions, upon request of any party, if the Dean or designee determines that such participation is essential to the resolution of a dispositive issue in the case.[9]

(j) The Dean or designee may permit a university official, and the mental health professional who prepared the evaluation, to appear at the informal hearing and to present evidence in support of any withdrawal recommendation.[10] Such evidence will not be presented by legal counsel for the University.

(k) The informal hearing shall be tape recorded by the Dean or designee. The tape(s) shall be kept with the pertinent case file for as long as the case file is maintained by the institution.

(l) A written decision shall be rendered by the Dean or designee within five business days after the completion of the informal hearing. The written decision, which should be mailed or personally delivered to the student, should contain a statement of reasons for any determination leading to involuntary withdrawal. The student should also be advised as to when a petition for reinstatement would be considered, along with any conditions for reinstatement.

---

[8]See generally, *Hart v. Ferris State* 557 F. Supp. 1379, 1385 (W.D. Mich., 1983).

[9]Routine cross-examination should not be permitted. Instead, the Dean or designee will need to be convinced that some critical issue (e.g. personal bias) could only be resolved through direct questioning at the informal hearing.

[10]This provision may be invoked in factually complicated cases when reliance upon a written evaluation may not be sufficient.

(m) The decision of the Dean or designee shall be final and conclusive and not subject to appeal.

DEVIATIONS FROM ESTABLISHED PROCEDURES[11]

14. Reasonable deviations from these procedures will not invalidate a decision or proceeding unless significant prejudice to a student may result.

---

[11]See *Winnick v. Manning,* 460 F.2d 545, 550 (2nd Cir. 1972). ("Minor" deviations not affecting "fundamental fairness" will be permitted).

Appendix II

Case Studies[1]

A. ANTHONY'S ROOMMATE

Anthony resides in a residence hall room with one other student. They are an unlikely pair. Anthony enjoys punk rock music; his roommate prefers the Andrews sisters. Anthony usually goes to bed around 3:30 a.m. and gets up at noon; his roommate is up at 6:30 a.m. in order to go jogging with his R.O.T.C. platoon. Anthony has long, textured, purple hair and wears an earring; his roommate has a crew cut and wears dog tags. As might be expected, Anthony finds this situation to be intolerable. He and his parents have complained to the Director of Residential Life.

The substance of Anthony's complaint is what he perceives to be the strange behavior of his roommate. His roommate never studies, is constantly engaged in body building, and frequently stages in mock "commando attacks" upon imaginary "enemy fortifications" outside the residence hall. He is also a reader of *Modern Mercenary* magazine, and a student of the martial arts. Among his more irritating activities, from Anthony's perspective, is the habit of staring at Anthony for hours at a time in what he calls "psychological warfare" exercises. Finally, Anthony is especially upset by his roommate's occasional hypnotic and rhythmic chanting of various battle songs and hymns during res-

---

[1] These case studies and the suggested responses are not designed to serve as comprehensive descriptions or models. Instead, they are intended for use as initial starting points for discussion, analysis, and criticism in training exercises. Such exercises would be most effective if conducted with participation by diverse staff members, including campus lawyers, administrators, therapists, and residence hall advisors. It would then be possible for employees with different responsibilities to better understand the perspectives of their colleagues. Ideally, when a crisis involving a student with an apparent mental disorder does arise, the staff would then be better able to work together as a team, in a spirit of mutual trust and cooperation. The importance of a "team" approach in responding to mental health emergencies has also been discussed by Tanner and Sewell (1979).

idence hall "quiet hours." Anthony, an avid reader of University regulations, is convinced that his roommate should be withdrawn from the university on "mental health" grounds.

Response

☐ In the absence of any violent acts, the use or display of any weapon, or the expression of any threat of violence, there does not appear to be any need to invoke any emergency procedure, such as interim withdrawal or suspension.

☐ It is by no means clear that Anthony's roommate may be suffering from a mental disorder, even if Anthony's version of the facts is accepted as accurate. A mandatory referral for psychological or psychiatric evaluation would be premature.

☐ An experienced staff member might spend some time reviewing the situation with Anthony. For example, Anthony should be asked if he has discussed any of his concerns and frustrations with his roommate. If not, he should be encouraged to do so. The staff member might monitor the situation to determine if Anthony has been successful in his efforts. At the same time, it would be prudent for the staff member to initiate some informal contact with Anthony's roommate. A primary concern would be the roommate's academic progress, his adjustment to campus life, and whether or not he has established any satisfying relationships with others.

☐ If Anthony and his roommate are unable to resolve their differences, a staff member might engage in structured mediation,[2] resulting in a behavioral "contract." For example, Anthony's roommate would be asked to agree to refrain from chanting during residence hall quiet hours. If the roommate's behavior continues, he may be found in violation of the residence hall agreement, or university disciplinary regulations, or both. Essentially, the charge against him would be that he intentionally engaged in disruptive behavior, preventing Anthony from studying or sleeping, in violation of published residence hall policies. Anthony's roommate might be placed on probation, assigned to community service, removed from the residence halls, or suspended from the university, if he persists in his misbehavior.

☐ It is possible, of course, that Anthony's roommate may modify his behavior only to the extent necessary to avoid any violation of published regulations. For example, knowing that Anthony hates mercenary magazines, the roommate might display them more prominently. Anthony is now witness to an unfortunate fact of life: we occasionally have to endure people whom we regard as

---

[2]See the Fall 1984 *Mediation Newsletter* (University of Massachusetts at Amherst) for a discussion of the role of resident advisors in conflict resolution.

nasty and irritating. The authorities are not able to rescue us, nor will we be permitted to inflict some illegal punishment of our own design. Instead, we can seek to change the attitudes of our antagonists, or simply devise personal strategies to control our own reactions to them.

☐ The decision not to withdraw Anthony's roommate on "mental health" grounds is premised upon an assumption that his interactions with staff members have revealed nothing more than eccentric behavior. Although he might profit from academic, personal, or career counseling, those forms of counseling should be made available on a voluntary basis. Likewise, it would be appropriate for residence hall officials to engage Anthony's roommate in ongoing discussion and dialogue about those aspects of his behavior which are offensive to others. Naturally, when such conversations occur, staff members might learn that the roommate's actions are more than merely eccentric. For example, he might display a consuming, irrational rage directed toward another individual or group, and manifest behavior which indicates that he is contemplating some form of violence. Under these circumstances, an immediate referral for evaluation (as well as a prompt warning to law enforcement authorities) would be necessary. In this regard, it will be important for staff members, including mental health professionals, to avoid giving absolute assurances of confidentiality. If Anthony's roommate poses an imminent danger to himself or the community, appropriate action should be taken in an effort to protect him or others (see, generally, *McIntosh*, 1979, pp. 512-513).

B. BAXTER AND HIS HISTORY PROFESSOR

Baxter is an unpleasant and contentious student who infuriates his community college history professor. Essentially, Baxter interrupts his professor and challenges every classroom assertion which the professor makes, usually with considerable gratuitous invective (e.g. "that's another biased and stupid statement, professor . . ..") Furthermore, Baxter giggles inappropriately in class, stands up and wanders about the room in the middle of lectures, and occasionally follows the professor across public areas of the campus, making unflattering remarks about the professor's clothing, as well as the professor's embarrassingly obvious toupee. The professor, who is convinced that Baxter has a mental disorder and may become violent, suggests that the mandatory withdrawal procedure be invoked.

Response

☐ As in the case of "Anthony's Roommate," (case study "A"), it would seem premature at this stage to refer Baxter for mandatory psychological or psychiatric evaluation, or to invoke an interim withdrawal. Instead, since some of Baxter's actions appear to constitute an intentional disruption of the classroom environment, he should be referred for possible disciplinary action. Baxter should also be given a letter from an appropriate campus official, informing him that he would be subject to interim disciplinary suspension (see Pavela, 1980, pp. 143-144) if further reports of classroom disruption are received.[3]

☐ The focus of any disciplinary action in Baxter's case would be on specific, disruptive acts (e.g. frequently interrupting the professor in class, without being called upon, and disturbing others by walking about the room, or making inappropriate noises). The lawful expression of an opinion, even if rude or unflattering to the professor, should not be subject to formal disciplinary action, although Baxter certainly could be challenged to find less abrasive ways to express himself.

☐ It will be important for the disciplinarian to listen carefully to Baxter's perspective, since Baxter's underlying misbehavior may be attributable, in part, to the professor's management of the classroom environment. For example, Baxter's anger and resentment may be the result of the professor's use of racially offensive language. While the professor's use of such language would not excuse Baxter, it might serve to mitigate any punishment. Furthermore, the professor's department chairperson, or other appropriate administrative officials, will wish to confer with the professor pertaining to any violation of professional or institutional standards.

☐ Regardless of Baxter's motivation, his proven misbehavior, in violation of published institutional standards,[4] will merit some disciplinary action. The nature of any sanction, however, would be influenced by Baxter's attitude and demeanor. The disciplinarian might make some assessment in that regard by engaging Baxter

---

[3]For example, such a letter might read:
"Dear Mr. ____:
We have received a report that you have violated Part nine (d) of the University *Code of Student Conduct*, as set forth on page three of the undergraduate catalog. Specifically, it is alleged that you intentionally disrupted the classroom of Professor ____, by repeatedly interrupting the professor without authorization, making inappropriate noises disturbing to other students, and walking about the room during the professor's lecture, all on November 5, 1984 at about 3 p.m. Please schedule an appointment for a preliminary interview, to be completed within five business days from the date of this letter. Also, it is important to understand that the University reserves the right to invoke an interim suspension, as permitted by Part fifteen of the *Code of Student Conduct*. Such suspension may be imposed immediately, without prior notice, if any further reports of classroom disruption are received by this office."

[4]For example, campus regulations may prohibit "intentionally or recklessly interfering with normal University or University sponsored activities, including, but not limited to, studying, teaching, research, University administration, or fire, police or emergency services" (see Pavela, 1980, p. 141).

in ethical dialogue. Such dialogue normally entails posing a series of questions, such as:

(1) Please tell me honestly, how would you feel if you were a professor, trying to teach a class, and a student behaved in the way you did yesterday?

(2) Granted that you feel you have a grievance against the professor, what would happen to the classroom environment across the campus if all students expressed a grievance in the way you did yesterday?

(3) What lawful ways are open to you to disagree with a professor, or challenge his or her conduct of the class?

The responses to these and other questions will enable the disciplinarian to fashion a penalty, as well as encourage Baxter to reflect about the process of ethical decision-making. For example, Baxter might appreciate that adherence to the "Golden Rule," and consideration of the generalized consequences of one's behavior, serve as intuitive and deductive starting points for examining ethical issues. Assuming that Baxter displays some genuine understanding of the wrongfulness of the behavior, it might be reasonable to place him on probationary status, premised upon his written commitment to avoid any further disruption of the classroom. Some variety of community service might also be assigned.

☐ If Baxter is returned to the class, it would be prudent for an experienced academic administrator to suggest ways in which the professor could minimize unproductive confrontations. For example, if Baxter has a profound policy disagreement with the professor, he could be given some opportunity to express contrary views in the classroom, perhaps in a short presentation, or a structured debate with another student. In any event, the professor's ability to display some sense of humor and perspective, along with a determination to refrain from replying in kind to invective or sarcasm, would contribute to a constructive resolution of the problem.

☐ It is possible, of course, that a disciplinary conference with Baxter may lead to a mandatory referral for psychological or psychiatric evaluation. For example, his expression of an intractable and unreasoning hostility toward the professor, coupled with ongoing disruptive behavior, might be grounds for such referral. However, even if it is determined after the evaluation that Baxter is suffering from a mental disorder, it would be better for him and the campus as a whole if he were removed from the institution on disciplinary grounds, unless he lacked the capacity to respond to the charges, or did not know the nature or wrongfulness of the conduct at the time of the offense.

CHARLES AND HIS CAT

Charles is a sensitive, introspective animal lover who lives in a residence hall where pets are expressly forbidden. He became deeply attached to "Rumpole," a large, languid, striped cat, which resident life employees ordered him to remove. Charles wrote a letter to the Director of Resident Life, stating that "Rumpole is my only friend. Since you are going to force me to get rid of him, my life isn't worth living. You will be responsible for what happens to me." Approximately twenty minutes after receiving the letter, the Director was informed that Charles had slashed his wrists, inflicting a number of superficial cuts.

Response

☐ Charles should be referred for mandatory evaluation. Appropriate local officials should also be contacted to determine if he should be committed to a state facility for observation. His parents should also be informed of the situation, unless the mental health professional responsible for the case advises to the contrary. (In accordance with the "Buckley Amendment," such contact with parents could be made without Charles' consent in an emergency, or if he is claimed by his parents as a dependent for tax purposes).

☐ An emergency or interim withdrawal from the University or the residence halls may not be necessary, depending on Charles' subsequent statements or behavior, and the availability of supportive friends or family members.

☐ To the extent that Charles' behavior is a matter of public knowledge in the residence hall, appropriate staff members might hold a number of informal discussions with concerned students. Essentially, the students should be informed that individuals who threaten or attempt to commit suicide are not automatically removed from the residence hall environment. Instead, reasonable efforts are made to allow such individuals to resume a normal life as part of the community. Specific ways in which interested students could contribute to this process might be suggested. Finally, any students who seem especially frightened or upset by the threatened or attempted suicide of another will merit individual attention from residence staff members, or trained counselors, as appropriate.

☐ While campus officials might reserve the right to delay implementation of a rule in an emergency, the threat of suicide should not prevent the reasonable enforcement of lawful campus regulations. Assuming that students who threaten or attempt to commit suicide are promptly referred for evaluation or observation by trained professionals, the reasonable enforcement of such regulations would not be grounds for legal liability. Consequently, in the present situation, a plan should be developed (in cooperation with the mental health professional responsible for the case, along with Charles' parents, if possible) leading to the eventual removal of "Rumpole" from the residence hall. Charles' response to such a plan may be an important factor in determining whether he will be allowed to remain in the hall, or at the university.

☐ It is possible that a mental health professional may determine that Charles is suffering from a mental disorder which is exacerbated in the academic environment. As a result, assuming it is likely that Charles will continue to engage in self-destructive behavior, he might be subject to mandatory withdrawal from the university. If he is withdrawn, Charles should be referred to an appropriate facility for observation and treatment.

☐ Some have suggested that suicidal students might be dismissed from the institution on disciplinary grounds. Such a practice will not be a viable option at many colleges and universities, since student and faculty members of the campus judiciary will be extremely reluctant to suspend or expel suicidal students who have not engaged in any other form of misbehavior. By analogy, in those remaining states where suicidal behavior might constitute a criminal offense, prosecutions are initiated rarely, if at all. This is so because one function of the criminal law, like campus disciplinary regulations, is to affirm community moral standards. Most decision-makers are simply not going to impose the moral condemnation associated with a criminal or disciplinary "conviction" in a case of attempted suicide, especially if the suicidal behavior was associated with a serious mental disorder.

D. DENNIS AND THE FALSE PROPHETS

Dennis, a resident student, frequently sits in the middle of the residence hall in a yoga position and stares at everyone who passes. He also burns incense, chants and calls for strength to rid the world of pagan religions and false prophets, and then goes door to door telling other residents that they are false prophets. There are signs painted on bathroom doors that "[t]he end is near for false prophets." Many residents on the floor are very nervous and fearful. Most have complained to the Resident Advisor.

The Residence Hall Director spoke to Dennis. Dennis simply stared at the Director and proclaimed "I don't talk to those who belong to pagan religions. You are a devil and a false prophet. Your end is near." The Director informed Dennis that others in the hall were nervous, could not study or sleep, and were even afraid to use the bathroom at night. Dennis did not respond, and left the Director's office.

The day after the meeting with the Director, Dennis was observed placing a sign on another student's room door that said "you are a false prophet and you cannot be allowed to continue your false ways. I commit my blood to put an end to your fake prophecies." There was blood smeared on the sign. The same day the Director received a blood stained hunting knife in the mail with a note that said "you are a false prophet."

Response

☐ No one can be certain that Dennis is responsible for all the incidents in question (e.g., another resident might have painted the signs on the bathroom doors, or mailed the knife to the Director). Nonetheless, based on Dennis' observed behavior, it would be reasonable to conclude that he may be suffering from a mental disorder. Furthermore, it would appear that Dennis may pose a danger of causing physical harm to himself or others. Under these circumstances, a referral for evaluation (see the sample policy at Appendix I) would be appropriate.

☐ Furthermore, Dennis was observed placing a blood smeared sign on another student's door. The circumstances indicate that Dennis may have engaged in self-destructive behavior, and has made what could reasonably be regarded as a threat of imminent violence. Also, Dennis' behavior is becoming increasingly disruptive. An interim withdrawal from the residence halls, or from the University, should be considered, along with civil commitment at a state facility for observation. Campus police should be informed.

☐ Dennis should also be charged with violating pertinent campus disciplinary regulations, as well as the residence hall occupancy agreement. For example, the campus disciplinary code might prohibit "intentionally or recklessly causing physical harm to any person on University premises or at University sponsored activities, or intentionally or recklessly causing reasonable apprehension of such harm" (Pavela, 1980, p. 141). The focus of any hearing would be whether Dennis "intentionally or recklessly" caused "reasonable apprehension" of "physical harm" to another member of the campus community. Other charges which might be filed could include the intentional and persistent disruption of the residence hall environment (e.g., burning incense in the public hallway; repeatedly knocking on doors and disturbing other residents, after being asked not to do so; placing a sign on another student's door, without authorization).

☐ It is possible that a mental health professional may determine that Dennis has a mental disorder. Such a finding, in itself, should not excuse Dennis from the disciplinary process. Instead, he should be diverted from the disciplinary system, and withdrawn on psychiatric grounds, only if he lacks the capacity to respond to the pending charges, or did not know the nature or wrongfulness of his conduct at the time of the offense.

☐ It will be important to avoid using the disciplinary process to punish Dennis for the expression of unpopular religious views. For example, the Residence Hall Director may have good reason to resent being called a devil, and the follower of a "pagan" religion. She might, when appropriate, inform Dennis that such remarks are offensive. If such an incident were to occur again, she could even require Dennis to leave her office. Nonetheless, Dennis should not be punished for the simple statement of an opinion. This issue frequently arises on campuses across the country, especially in the context of religious or racial epithets. The problem was addressed by a Yale University committee in 1975. The committee, chaired by the historian C. Vann Woodward, concluded that:

> [s]hock, hurt, and anger are not consequences to be weighed lightly. No member of the community with a decent respect for others should use, or encourage others to use, slurs and epithets intended to discredit another's race, ethnic group, religion, or sex . . . [But] even when some members of the university community fail to meet their social and ethical responsibilities, the paramount obligation of the university is to protect their right to free expression. If the university's overriding commitment to free expression is to be sustained, secondary social and ethical responsibilities must be left to the informal processes of suasion, example and argument (Report, p. 18).

E. EDWARD AND HIS GIRLFRIEND

Edward is a twenty-seven-year-old graduate student in computer science. He used to spend as much as eighteen hours a day in the computer science center, and was devoted to his work. Edward was also lonely, and very much wished that he had some significant relationship with a woman.

Edward's dreams were answered when Denise, an eighteen-year-old freshman, came to the computer science center for tutoring. She liked Edward's shy, retiring manner, and began seeing him socially. However, after three weeks, she sent Edward a short note, explaining that she had met another man and wanted to be "just friends."

Edward was crushed. Denise was his first girlfriend, and stirred deep emotions in him. He called her home daily, often late at night, and would not stop doing so, even after Denise angrily told him to leave her alone. Furthermore, Edward would follow Denise about the campus, trying to talk with her on every possible occasion. One time, he blocked the door of Denise's car, delaying her departure from the University, while he implored her to resume their relationship. Edward would also send erotic poetry to Denise through the campus computer, persisted in giving her expensive gifts, and regularly called Denise's mother to ask about Denise's social life. Finally, the past two weekends, Edward has been observed in his car, parked outside Denise's home (approximately eighteen miles from campus), waiting for Denise to return from her evenings out with her new boyfriend.

Denise and her parents are convinced that Edward has a mental disorder, that his condition is getting worse, and that he may be contemplating some form of violence. They demand immediate action.

Response

☐ It would be prudent for Denise and her parents to contact the local police and to inform them of the situation. Campus police should also be notified. Furthermore, the local telephone company might be advised of Edward's persistent, late night telephone calls.

☐ Denise and her parents are entirely justified in asking for assistance in this matter. Nonetheless, it would be premature to assume that Edward has a mental disorder, or that some sort of psychiatric evaluation or withdrawal procedure should be invoked. Instead, preliminary consideration should be given to the likelihood that Edward is an immature, inexperienced, and somewhat eccentric young man, who is simply bewildered by his first infatuation.

☐ Edward appears to have committed at least two disciplinary violations: physical interference with Denise's freedom of movement on campus (i.e., blocking her car door), and misuse of University computer facilities to send erotic poetry to her. The latter is not a form of protected "free speech," since campus officials may impose reasonable time, place, and manner restrictions upon expressive activity (see Gehring, D. (Ed.), 1983, pp. 16-18). Edward should be notified of the appropriate charges and referred for an immediate interview with a disciplinary officer.

☐ An experienced disciplinary officer, as an intelligent lay observer, can make some assessment of Edward's attitude and demeanor. Assuming that Edward does not dispute the basic facts, it will be important to know if he understands the nature of his misbehavior, has the capacity to express any genuine regret for the difficulties he has caused, and if he plans to conduct himself differently in the future. If Edward manifests a positive response, it should be possible to resolve his case through the disciplinary process.

☐ Before taking any final action, it would be wise for the disciplinarian to discuss the matter with Denise. She may be concerned about Edward's reaction to the imposition of discipline, and might be invited to review the options available to the disciplinarian. One of the options in these circumstances would be a form of "pre-sentence probation," in which Edward would enter into a written agreement to refrain from certain specified acts in the future (e.g., calling Denise or her mother on the telephone, waiting outside Denise's home, etc.). Further action upon the pending charges could then be deferred, pending subsequent review of Edward's adherence to the agreement.

☐ The disciplinarian should also discuss with Denise how she might contribute to a constructive resolution of the problem. It is entirely possible that she may be inexperienced in these situations, and might be making a number of errors in judgment. For example, should she continue to accept gifts from Edward, she could be informed that Edward interprets such behavior as an indication that she wishes to resume their former relationship. The disciplinarian may be in the unique position of being able to talk to both parties in this matter and should take full advantage of that opportunity to correct any misimpressions which might have arisen on either side.

☐ Finally, the imposition of discipline does not preclude offering some sort of professional assistance to Edward. He might be encouraged, on a voluntary basis, to make an appointment at the counseling center. His difficulties with relationships are certainly not unique, and he might even be willing to discuss them with others in the context of group therapy. Nonetheless, since Edward has violated the campus code of student conduct, the primary responsibility for responding to his behavior does fall to the discipline office.

F. FRANCES AND HER DIET

Frances is a shy, unusually intelligent 19 year-old student who lives in a residence hall suite with two other women at a small, private university. Frances has no known friends in the residence hall, and spends the bulk of her free time alone. However, she has initiated a counseling relationship with a university psychologist, who is treating her for anorexia nervosa.

Frances' eating disorder is becoming increasingly serious, and is alarming her roommates, as well as her psychologist. Nonetheless, she stubbornly refuses to adhere to her treatment plan, which includes a diet with a specified level of caloric intake, to be monitored through a daily journal. Frances does recognize that she has an eating disorder, but strongly disagrees with her psychologist as to the severity of the problem.

The psychologist treating Frances has concluded that Frances' physical condition is becoming life threatening. He sent her to the attending physician, who requested that she submit to immediate hospitalization. Frances refused, and threatened to break off the therapeutic relationship. The psychologist, who considered state involuntary commitment procedures to be inadequate under the circumstances, called the Dean of Students and requested that Frances be informed that she must seek immediate medical attention, or be withdrawn from the university. Frances vehemently protested the psychologist's action, and considered it a breach of their confidential relationship.

Response

☐ The Dean should consider the psychologist's recommendation. The information provided by the psychologist did not constitute an ethical breach of confidentiality,[5] since release of the information was necessary to prevent a substantial risk of immediate harm to the client. Furthermore, Counseling Center policy in this regard was distributed in writing to the client in advance. The policy stated, in part, that:

"[t]he counseling center takes every reasonable precaution to protect your privacy. The identity of those using our services, along with the personally identifiable disclosures made in the course of the counseling relationship, will be regarded as confidential. Confidential information will not be shared with parties outside the counseling center, without your express, written consent, unless there is a clear and imminent danger to an individual or to society. However, if you are referred for evaluation, in accordance with applicable university procedures, you should understand that the evaluation will be shared with the appropriate university official requesting the evaluation."

☐ It would be prudent for the psychologist to seek to invoke state involuntary commitment procedures in a serious mental health emergency, even if those procedures had been cumbersome and ineffective in the past. This is so because reliance upon such procedures may constitute a "generally accepted standard of professional conduct" in the eyes of the law. Whenever possible, the parents of a student should be consulted about such a decision,

---

[5]See Principle Five, "Confidentiality" in *Ethical Principles of Psychologists* (American Psychological Association, 1981):

psychologists have a primary obligation to respect the confidentiality of information obtained from persons in the course of their work as psychologists. They reveal such information to others only with the consent of the person or the person's legal representative, except in those unusual circumstances in which not to do so would result in clear danger to the person or to others. Where appropriate, psychologists inform their clients of the legal limits of confidentiality.

since they may seek to arrange for appropriate, alternative treatment. Nonetheless, emergency referral to a state mental health facility, in accordance with an applicable state statute or regulation, may not require parental permission.

☐ Assuming that state involuntary commitment procedures were not effective in Frances' case, and that she persists in refusing medical treatment as her health deteriorates, she should be informed that the university will invoke its involuntary withdrawal policy. Ideally, if time permits, the threatened invocation of such a policy might induce Frances to obtain the treatment which could stabilize her condition. The university may then delay any decision to withdraw her, pending further evaluation of her ability and willingness to follow a reasonable treatment plan.

☐ If all else fails, the university should withdraw Frances, in accordance with the applicable involuntary withdrawal policy. An additional effort should be made to invoke state involuntary commitment procedures, on the ground that Frances' condition has continued to deteriorate. Unless the mental health professional responsible for the case advises to the contrary, Frances' parents should be contacted immediately. Finally, Frances should be informed in writing that the university does not have the facilities or resources to treat her condition, and that she is advised to seek immediate medical attention. Appropriate facilities where such treatment might be obtained should be specifically identified.

☐ The tragic fact in this situation is that Frances may die as a result of her eating disorder. The university should be able to document all of the steps which have been taken to assist her. The final decision to withdraw Frances was not motivated by the thoughtless compulsion to "dump" a student in serious mental or physical jeopardy. Instead, the university made a reasonable effort to use all of its available resources, including threatened invocation of the withdrawal policy itself, to induce Frances to cooperate in an appropriate treatment plan. Finally, it was necessary for university officials to consider the impact of Frances' behavior and condition upon other students, including her roommates. The university should expect students to accept and appreciate a considerable degree of eccentricity among members of a diverse community. It would not be reasonable, however, to be indifferent to the concerns of students who were placed in an environment in which they had little choice but to watch another individual slowly starve herself to death.

G. GERRY AND THE L.S.D.

Gerry is an eighteen-year-old freshman who lives in a residence hall reserved for honor students at a public college. One evening, she and her roommate ordered a pizza. When the pizza arrived, Gerry produced a large kitchen knife and proceeded to cut the pizza into smaller sections. Then, while her roommate was distracted at the other end of the table, Gerry walked behind the roommate and stabbed her, causing a serious wound requiring lengthy hospitalization. There had been no prior history of violence between the two women, who had regarded each other as close friends.

Gerry was promptly arrested and held in the county detention center for two days, until her parents paid the $10,000 bail set by a local magistrate. Her parents also obtained the services of a prominent criminal lawyer. The lawyer's strategy in the case was to assert that Gerry's behavior was the result of her first time experimentation with L.S.D., shortly after she arrived at the college. The L.S.D. reportedly produced a delayed hallucinatory experience, in which Gerry believed her roommate was planning to harm her by spreading poisonous mushrooms on the pizza. Gerry's lawyer expected to be successful in delaying her criminal trial for several months, and obtained a statement from a psychiatrist, who asserted that Gerry's hallucinatory experiences could be controlled with proper medication. Remarkably, the lawyer also secured the support of the victim, who wrote a forgiving testimonial in Gerry's behalf. Finally, Gerry's lawyer contacted the Dean of Students and stated that Gerry would now be returning to her residence hall room and resuming her studies. He cautioned the Dean that any administrative or disciplinary action taken against his client would be challenged on the ground that Gerry was a "handicapped" person, as defined by Section 504 of the Rehabilitation Act of 1973. Furthermore, it was the lawyer's contention, given the upcoming criminal trial, that any administrative or disciplinary action would constitute a form of double jeopardy, prohibited by the fifth and fourteenth amendments to the United States Constitution.

Response

☐ The Dean should not respond to the lawyer without conferring with counsel for the university. In turn, counsel for the university will normally wish to inform the county or state prosecutor of any plan to conduct a disciplinary hearing prior to the scheduled criminal trial. The university may be agreeable to delaying a disciplinary hearing if the prosecutor makes a convincing argument that such a hearing would significantly jeopardize the criminal case. In turn, the prosecutor needs to understand that delays in bringing the case to trial will produce extraordinary tensions in an environment where witnesses, defendants and victims must live, work and study in close proximity to each other.

☐ This case highlights the need for a fair and efficient disciplinary process designed to protect the campus community. In many jurisdictions, the criminal justice system is deficient in bringing cases to trial in a timely manner.[6] All too often, criminal cases are scheduled at the convenience of lawyers, without sufficient regard for important social interests, as well as the interests of the accused. Accordingly, it might be advisable to state directly in the campus disciplinary code that:

> [s]tudents may be accountable to both civil authorities and to the university for acts which constitute violations of law and of this code. Disciplinary action at the University will normally proceed during the pendency of criminal proceedings and will not be subject to challenge on the ground that criminal charges involving the same incident have been dismissed or reduced (Pavela, 1980, p. 141).

☐ The argument raised by Gerry's lawyer pertaining to Section 504 of the Rehabilitation Act should be rejected. Gerry can be expected to abide by the same reasonable disciplinary standards as other students, even though she may be suffering from a mental disorder. The college would not be discriminating against Gerry "solely" because she had a handicap. Instead, the college is simply enforcing reasonable rules and regulations which Gerry is expected to follow *in spite of* any handicap (see, generally, *Southeastern Community College*, 1979; *Doe*, 1981).

☐ A college disciplinary hearing is administrative or "civil" in nature. The double jeopardy clause of the Fifth Amendment applies to being tried twice in *criminal* cases. Gerry's lawyer surely knows he is making a specious argument, since a doctor, lawyer or other professional who commits a criminal offense can also be subject to disciplinary proceedings pertaining to the same incident, conducted by a state licensing agency. College students are in an analogous position, since they are being trained to assume positions of trust and responsibility in the larger society. It is reasonable for a college or university to enforce its own disciplinary rules, precisely because college and university students can be expected to adhere to a higher standard of behavior.

---

[6]A recent example from the October 16, 1984 *Washington Post* (p. c3) highlights the problem:

> [a] Southeast Washington man who is accused of last week's rape of a 10-year-old girl as she walked near an elementary school had been free for more than two years as he waited to be tried on an unrelated charge of assault with intent to commit robbery, according to D.C. Superior Court records.
>
> Joe Anthony Barber Jr., 27, charged with rape while armed in last Thursday's incident, has appeared in court 13 times before five different judges since his arrest on Sept. 9, 1982, on the earlier assault charge, records show.
>
> Since his indictment in that case on October 20, 1982, Barber's trial date has been postponed six times and he has been represented by four different court-appointed lawyers, according to court records."

Similarly, the *New York Times* recently reported that "criminal cases take over a year to go to trial" in New York City (January 14, 1985, p. B3).

☐ Nor would there be any validity to an assertion made by Gerry's lawyer that it would somehow violate Gerry's rights if a disciplinary hearing were scheduled before her criminal trial. This argument was effectively discredited by the Vermont Supreme Court in *Nzuve* (1975):

[d]iscipline imposed by the academic community need not await the outcome of other proceedings. We conceive that holding to be more in line with our own ideals of fairness and the balancing of all interests involved. Educational institutions have both a need and a right to formulate their own standards and to enforce them; such enforcement is only coincidentally related to criminal charges and the defense against them. To hold otherwise would, in our view, lead logically to the conclusion that civil remedies must, as a matter of law, wait for determination until related criminal charges are disposed of. By parallel, the owner of stolen property could not obtain damages or its recovery until criminal prosecution had been completed. Similarly, in the instant case, the complaining witness could not have redress for the assault on her, if proven, until the pending criminal charges had run their long course of trial and appeal. Nor would it be at all unusual for the temporary relief here sought to enable the plaintiff to complete his education, thus effectively completing an 'end run' around the disciplinary rules and procedures of the college (p. 325).

☐ Gerry's lawyer would also be in error if he contended that Gerry would have a Fifth Amendment right to remain silent in a college disciplinary proceeding. It is entirely reasonable for the college to expect Gerry to respond to relevant questions raised at her hearing, since ethical discussion, confrontation and dialogue should be a part of the disciplinary process in an educational setting. Furthermore, to protect the interests of students in Gerry's position, campus disciplinary regulations should state that the hearing panel could draw a negative inference from a refusal to speak, which might result in suspension or expulsion. If a student then elected to answer, the answer could not be used against him or her in the subsequent criminal case (see *Goldberg*, 1967; *Furutani*, 1969; *Nzuve*, 1975; *Hart*, 1983).

☐ Having considered and rejected the initial objections raised by Gerry's lawyer, the college may process the disciplinary case, as follows:

(a) An appropriate campus administrator may elect to invoke an immediate, interim suspension, in accordance with campus disciplinary regulations. At the same time, the official may refer Gerry for evaluation, pursuant to college standards and procedures for involuntary withdrawal on psychological or psychiatric grounds. Gerry might be reinstated, pending her disciplinary hearing, depending upon the outcome of the evaluation.

(b) Just as the administrator was expected to use unbiased judgment in electing to refer Gerry for evaluation, the mental health professional conducting the evaluation should be expected to follow the evaluative standard set forth in applicable institutional policies (see Appendix I). Consequently, if Gerry is capable of responding to the pending disciplinary charges, and knew the nature and wrongfulness of her action at the time of the offense, her case should be processed through the disciplinary system, even if she might be suffering from a mental disorder.

(c) Given the facts as set forth in the hypothetical, it is likely that Gerry's case should be referred for a disciplinary hearing. Gerry apparently knew the nature of the act, since she knowingly and intentionally stabbed her roommate. Also, it could not be said that Gerry, as a result of mental disorder, was somehow rendered unaware of the wrongfulness of the behavior, since even her "hallucination," if true, would not have justified the immediate use of potentially deadly force in self-defense.

Table of Cases

Figueroa v. State, 604 *P.* 2d 1198 (Hawaii, 1979).

Furutani v. Ewigleben, 297 *F. Supp.* 1163 (N.D. Cal., 1969).

Gabrilowitz v. Newman, 582 *F.* 2d 100 (1st Cir., 1978).

Glassman v. New York Medical College, 315 *N.Y.S.* 2d 1 (Sup., 1970).

Goldberg v. Regents of University of California, 57 *Cal. Rptr.* 463 (Cal. App., 1967).

Goss v. Lopez, 419 *U.S.* 565 (1975).

Greenhill v. Bailey, 519 *F.* 2d 5 (8th Cir., 1975).

Hall v. Board of Supervisors, Southern University, 405 *So.* 2d 1125 (La. Ct. App., 1981).

Hart v. Ferris State College, 557 *F. Supp.* 1379 (W.D. Mich., 1983).

Healy v. James, 408 *U.S.* 169 (1972) (Douglas, J., concurring).

Henson v. Honor Committee of U.Va., 719 *F.* 2d 69 (4th Cir., 1983).

In Re Gault, 387 *U.S.* 1 (1967).

In Re Sealy, 218 *So.* 2d 765 (Fla. Dist. Ct. App., 1969).

Jesik v. Maricopa County Community College District, 611 *P.* 2d 547 (Ariz., 1980).

Johnson v. State, 447 *P.* 2d 352 (Cal., 1968).

Jones v. State Board of Education, 279 *F. Supp.* 190 (M.D. Tenn., 1968); *aff'd*, 407 *F.* 2d 834 (6th Cir., 1969); *cert. granted*, 396 *U.S.* 817 (1969); *cert. dismissed*, 397 *U.S.* 31 (1970).

Keene v. Rodgers, 316 *F. Supp.* 217 (D. Me. 1970).

Leedy v. Hartnett, 510 *F. Supp.* 1125 (M.D. Pa., 1981), *aff'd*, 676 *F.* 2d 686 (3rd Cir., 1982).

Lipari v. Sears Roebuck & Co., 497 *F. Supp.* 185 (D. Neb., 1980).

Lombard v. Board of Education of the City of New York, 502 *F.* 2d 631 (2nd Cir., 1974), *cert. denied*, 420 *U.S.* 976 (1975).

Lynch v. Baxley, 386 *F. Supp.* 378 (M.D. Ala., 1974), rev'd on other grounds, 651 *F.* 2d 387 (5th Cir., 1981).

Maricopa County v. Cowart, 471 *P.* 2d 265 (Ariz., 1970).

Marshall v. Maguire, 424 *N.Y.S.* 2d 89 (1980).

Mathews v. Eldridge, 424 *U.S.* 319 (1976).

McDonald v. Board of Trustees of the University of Illinois, 375 *F. Supp.* 95 (N.D. Ill., 1974), *aff'd.* 503 *F.* 2d 105 (7th Cir., 1974).

McIntosh v. Milano, 403 *A.* 2d 500 (N.J. Super., 1979).

Miller v. State, 478 *N.Y.S.* 2d 829 (N.Y., 1984).

Morale v. Grigel, 422 *F. Supp.* 988 (D.N.H., 1976).

Moresco v. Clark case #45523 Supreme Court of New York, Appellate Division, Third Department, 1984 (see June, 1984 *The College Student and the Courts* pp. 573-574).

Morris v. Slappy, 461 *U.S.* 1 (1983).

Mullins v. Pine Manor College, 449 *N.E.* 2d 331 (Mass., 1983).

Nancy P. v. Trustees of Indiana State University, No. 81-7-C (S.D. Ind., 1981) (Temporary restraining order issued January 23, 1981).

Napolitano v. Trustees of Princeton University, 453 *A.* 2d 279, *aff'd* 453 *A.* 2d 263 (N.J. Super, 1982).

National Union of Marine Cooks and Stewards v. Arnold 348 *U.S.* 37 (1954).

New York State Association for Retarded Children v. Carey, 612 *F.* 2d 644 (2nd Cir., 1979).

North v. Board of Trustees of the University of Illinois, 27 *N.E.* 54, (Ill., 1891).

Nzuve v. Castleton State College, 335 A. 2d 321 (Vt., 1975).

O'Connor v. Donaldson, 422 U.S. 563 (1975).

Parham v. J.R., 442 U.S. 584 (1979).

Petersen v. State, 671 P. 2d 230 (Wash., 1983).

Peterson v. San Francisco Community College District, 205 Cal. Rptr. 842 (Cal., 1984).

Petrey v. Flaugher, 505 F. Supp. 1087 (E.D. Ky., 1981).

Pushkin v. Regents of the University of Colorado, 658 F. 2d 1372 (10th Cir., 1981).

Racine Unified School District v. Thompson, 321 N.W. 2d 334 (Wisc., 1982).

Reetz v. Michigan, 188 U.S. 505 (1903).

Relyea v. State, 385 So. 2d 1378 (Fla. App., 1980).

Rennie v. Klein, 653 F. 2d 836 (3rd Cir., 1981).

Roberts v. United States, 445 U.S. 552 (1980).

Semler v. Psychiatric Institute of Washington, D.C., 538 F. 2d 121 (4th Cir., 1976), cert. denied, 429 U.S. 827 (1976).

Setrin v. Glassboro State College, 346 A. 2d 102 (N.J. Super., 1975).

Shamloo v. Mississippi State Board of Trustees, 620 F. 2d 516 (5th Cir., 1980).

Shaw v. Glickman, 415 A. 2d 625 (Md. App., 1980).

Smith v. United States, 437 F. Supp. 1004 (E.D. Pa., 1977).

Smyth v. Lubbers, 398 F. Supp. 777 (W.D. Mich., 1975).

Sneider v. Hyatt Corp., 390 F. Supp. 976 (N.D. Ga., 1975).

Soglin v. Kauffman, 295 F. Supp. 978 (W.D. Wis., 1968) aff'd 418 F. 2d 163 (7th Cir., 1969).

Sohmer v. Kinnard, 535 F. Supp. 50 (D. Md., 1982).

Southeastern Community College v. Davis, 442 U.S. 397 (1979).

Speake v. Grantham, 317 F. Supp. 1253 (S.D. Miss., 1970), aff'd 440 F. 2d 1351 (5th Cir., 1971).

Steier v. New York Education Commissioner, 271 F. 2d 13 (2nd Cir., 1959).

Tarasoff v. Regents of the University of California, 551 P. 2d 334 (Cal., 1976).

Tedeschi v. Wagner College, 427 N.Y.S. 2d 760 (N.Y., 1980).

Thompson v. County of Alameda, 614 P. 2d 728 (Cal., 1980).

Tinker v. Des Moines School District, 393 U.S. 503 (1968).

Turof v. Kibbee, 527 F. Supp. 880 (E.D. N.Y., 1981).

Underwood v. United States, 356 F. 2d 92 (5th Cir., 1966).

United States v. Bohle, 445 F. 2d 54 (7th Cir., 1971).

United States v. Grayson, 438 U.S. 41 (1978).

Uzzell v. Friday, 592 F. Supp. 1502 (M.D. N.C., 1984).

Vitek v. Jones, 445 U.S. 480 (1980).

Wasson v. Trowbridge, 382 F. 2d 807 (2nd Cir., 1967).

Wellner v. Minnesota State Junior College Board, 487 F. 2d 153 (8th Cir., 1973).

West Virginia State Board of Education v. Barnette, 319 U.S. 624 (1943).

Wilson v. Continental Insurance Cos., 274 N.W. 2d 679 (Wisc., 1979).

Winnick v. Manning, 460 F. 2d 545 (2nd Cir., 1972).

Wisconsin v. Constantineau, 400 U.S. 433 (1971).

Woods v. Simpson, 126 *A.* 882 (Md.,
1924).

Wright v. Texas Southern University,
392 *F.* 2d 728 (5th Cir., 1968).

Yench v. Stockmar, 483 *F.* 2d 820
(10th Cir., 1973).

Zanders v. Louisiana State Board of
Education, 281 *F. Supp.* 747 (W.D.
La., 1968).

Bibliography

áKempis, T. (1925). *The Imitation of Christ.* London: Whytford.

Adebimpe, V. (1981, March). Overview: White Norms and Psychiatric Diagnosis of Black Patients. *The American Journal of Psychiatry*, 279-285.

Alvarez, A. (1973). *The Savage God: A Study of Suicide*, New York: Bantam.

American Psychiatric Association (1977). *Confidentiality and Third Parties.* Washington, D.C.: Author.

American Psychiatric Association (1980). *Diagnostic and Statistical Manual of Mental Disorders* (DSM-III). Washington, D.C. Author.

American Psychiatric Association (1981, June 1). Amicus brief filed in *Estelle* v. *Smith* 451 *U.S.* 454 (1981), cited in the *National Law Journal*, 5.

American Psychological Association (1981). *Ethical Principles of Psychologists.* Washington, D.C.: Author.

American Psychological Association (1978). *Report of the Task Force on the Role of Psychology in the Criminal Justice System.* Washington, D.C.: Author.

Anred Alert (1983, June). Eugene, Ore.: Anorexia Nervosa and Related Eating Disorders, Inc.

Barton, W.E. (1968). Diagnosis by Mail. *American Journal of Psychiatry, 124,* 1446-48.

Bemis, K. (1978). Current Approaches to the Etiology and Treatment of Anorexia Nervosa. *Psychological Bulletin, 85,* 593-617.

Berger, R. (1977). *Government by Judiciary.* Cambridge: Harvard University Press.

Bernard, M.L., & Bernard, J.L. (1980, March). Institutional Responses to the Suicidal Student: Ethical and Legal Considerations. *Journal of College Student Personnel*, 109-113.

Bernard, M.L., & Bernard, J.L. (1982, September). Factors Related to Suicidal Behavior Among College Students and the Impact of Institutional Response. *Journal of College Student Personnel*, 409-413.

Blaine, G., & Carmen, L. (1968, December). Causal Factors in Suicidal Attempts by Male and Female College Students. *American Journal of Psychiatry*, 146-149.

Bower, B. (1984, June 1). Predicting Dangerousness: Future Imperfect. *Science News*, 365-367.

Braunstein, D. (1982). Custodial Suicide Cases: An Analytical Approach to Determine Liability for Wrongful Death. *Boston University Law Review, 62*, 177-213.

Brenner, M. (1980, June). Bulimarexia. *Savvy*, 54-59.

Brody, J. (1984, January 17). A Broader New View of Victim's Psychology Reported. *New York Times*, C1.

Chase, I. (1972, August 5). Cited in The Eagleton Affair: Stigma of Mental Disorder. *Science News*, 85.

Chickering, A. (1969). *Education and Identity*. San Francisco: Jossey-Bass.

Cocozza, J., & Steadman, H. (1978, February). Prediction in Psychiatry: An Example of Misplaced Confidence in Experts. *Social Problems*, 265-276.

Daily Collegian. (1980, October 10). Univ. of Massachusetts at Amherst, 1.

Davis, K. (1971). *Discretionary Justice*. Urbana: Illini Books.

Dershowitz, A. (1970). The Law on Dangerousness: Some Fictions About Predictions. *Journal of Legal Education, 23*, 24-49.

de Saint Exupery, A. (1942). Flight to Arras in *Airman's Odyssey*. New York: Cornwall.

de Saint Exupery, A. (1942). Wind, Sand and Stars, in *Airman's Odyssey*. New York: Cornwall.

Dewey, J. (1951). *Reconstruction in Philosophy*. Boston: Beacon.

Diamond, B. (1974). The Psychiatric Prediction of Dangerousness. *University of Pennsylvania Law Review, 123*, 439-452.

Eccles, J., & Robinson, D. (1984). *Our Brain and Our Mind*. New York: MacMillan.

Eddy, E. (1977, Winter). What Happened to Student Values? *Educational Record*, 7-16.

Ennis, B.J., & Litwack, T.R. (1974). Psychiatry and the Presumption of Expertise, Flipping Coins in the Courtroom. *California Law Review, 62*, 693-752.

Enright, A., & Sansone, R. (1983, April-June). Therapeutic Alternatives in the Treatment of Eating Disorders. National Anorexic Aid Society, *Newsletter*, 1-4.

Fleming, J., & Maximov, B. (1974). The Patient or His Victim: The Therapist's Dilemma. *California Law Review, 62*, 1025-1068.

Fleming, R.W. (1976, January 15). University of Michigan Memorandum addressed to "Deans, Directors, and Department Chairpersons."

Foucault, M. (1973). *Madness and Civilization*. New York: Vintage.

Frankl, V. (1978). *The Unheard Cry for Meaning*. New York: Simon and Schuster.

Fromm, E. (1964). *The Heart of Man*. New York: Harper and Row.

Gaylin, W. (1982). *The Killing of Bonnie Garland*. New York: Simon and Schuster.

Gehring, D. (1983, Winter). The Dismissal of Students with Serious Emotional Problems: An Administrative Decision Model. *NASPA Journal*, 9-14.

Gehring, D. (Ed.). (1983) *Administering College and University Housing: A Legal Perspective*. Asheville, N.C.: College Administration Publications, Inc.

Geiger, G. (1947). *Philosophy and the Social Order*. Cambridge, Mass.: Riverside.

Greenberg, D. (1974). Involuntary Psychiatric Commitments to Prevent Suicide. *N.Y.U.L. Review*, 49, 227-269.

Gross, M. (1978). *The Psychological Society*. New York: Random House.

Halvorson, P. (1983, January 24). Personal communication to author.

Hoffman, J. (1979). *Ethical Confrontation in Counseling*. Chicago: University of Chicago Press.

Joint Statement on Rights and Freedoms of Students. (1967). Joint Commission on Rights and Freedoms of Students. Washington, D.C.: American Association of University Professors.

Kahle, L.R., & Sales, B.D. (1978, August). Attitudes of Clinical Psychologists Toward Involuntary Civil Commitment Law. *Professional Psychology*, 428-439.

Kaplin, W. (1978). *The Law of Higher Education*. San Francisco: Jossey-Bass.

Kenniston, K. (1971). *Youth and Dissent*. New York: Harcourt.

Kirp, D.L. (1976). Proceduralism and Bureaucracy: Due Process in the School Setting. *Stanford Law Review*, 26, 841-876.

Knuth, M. (1979). Civil Liability for Causing or Failing to Prevent Suicide. *Loyola of Los Angeles Law Review*, 12, 967-999.

Kress, F. (1979). Evaluations of Dangerousness. *Schizophrenia Bulletin*, 5, 211-217.

LaBier, D. (1983, June 28). Perspective: Shrinking the Shrinks. *Washington Post*, C5.

Lamont, L. (1979). *Campus Shock*. New York: Dutton.

Lasch, C. (1979). *The Culture of Narcissism*. New York: Warner.

Lasch, C. (1984, February 2). The Great American Variety Show. *New York Review of Books*, 34-40.

Lippmann, W. (1929). *A Preface to Morals*. New York: MacMillan.

Levine, A. (1981). *When Dreams and Heroes Died*. San Francisco: Jossey-Bass.

Litman, R. Cited in Schneidman, E., & Mandelkorn, P. (1970). *Psychology of Suicide*. New York: Science House.

Lucas, A. (1978, August). Anorexia Nervosa. *Comtemporary Nutrition*, 1-2.

Melick, K. (1983, April 28). Program Administrator, National Anorexic Aid Society, Inc. Personal communication to author.

Menninger, K. (1959, August). Verdict Guilty, Now What? *Harper's Magazine*, 60-64; cited in Murphy, J. (1973). *Punishment and Rehabilitation*. Belmont, Ca.: Wadsworth.

Menninger, K. (1973). *Whatever Became of Sin?* New York: Hawthorn.

Mental Health Update. (1984, Spring). University of Maryland Health Center *Newsletter*, 1-4.

Moore, M. (1984). *Law and Psychiatry*. Cambridge: Cambridge University Press.

Morgan, D. (1981, December 27). The Search for Young Americans for Something to Call Their Own. *Washington Post* A1, A16.

Morris, H. (1981, October). A Paternalistic Theory of Punishment. *American Philosophical Quarterly*, 263-271.

Morris, N. (1983). *Madness and the Criminal Law*. Chicago: University of Chicago Press.

Niebuhr, R. (1965). *Man's Nature and His Communities*. New York: Scribners.

Note, Torts. (1961). Liability for Suicide—Guidance Counselor Held Not Responsible. *University of Wisconsin Law Review*, (1961), pp. 517-522.

Pavela, G. (1980). Limiting the Pursuit of Perfect Justice on Campus. *Journal of College and University Law*, 6, 137-160.

Pavela, G. (1982-83). Therapeutic Paternalism and the Misuse of Mandatory Psychiatric Withdrawals on Campus. *Journal of College and University Law*, 9, 101-141.

Pavela, G. (1983, January 26). Sanctions for Student Misbehavior: Let the Punishment Fit the Crime. *Chronicle of Higher Education*, 32.

Peck, M. (1984, March 4). Cited in J. Brody, The Haunting Specter of Teen-Age Suicide. *New York Times*, 8E.

Perry, W. (1981). Cognitive and Ethical Growth. In A. Chickering (Ed.), *The Modern American College*. San Francisco: Jossey-Bass.

Plato (1960). *Gorgias*. (Hamilton, Trans.). New York: Penguin.

Procedures for Certain Student Cases Involving Psychiatric Issues, University of Virginia, (undated).

Rachlin, S., Halpern, A., & Portnow, S. (1984, Feb.). The Volitional Rule, Personality Disorders and the Insanity Defense. *Psychiatric Annals*, 139-147.

Restak, R. (1983, March 23). They Sue Psychiatrists, Don't They? *Washington Post*, A25.

Rigotti, N. (1984, December 20). Exercise for Anorexia. *Washington Post*, A8.

Report of the Committee on Freedom of Expression at Yale University. Cited in the *New York Times*, January 26, 1975, p. 18.

Robinson, D. (1970). Consultant's Report, *Working Papers of the National Commission on Reform of Federal Criminal Laws*. Washington, D.C.: U.S. Government Printing Office.

Rosenhan, D. (1973, January 19). On Being Sane in Insane Places. *Science*, 250-257.

Rubel, J. (1983, January 18). President, Anorexia Nervosa and Related Eating Disorders, Inc. Personal communication to author.

Rubin, B. (1972). Prediction of Dangerousness in Mentally Ill Criminals. *Archives General Psychiatry, 27*, 397-407.

Samenow, S. (1984). *Inside the Criminal Mind.* New York: Times Books.

Sawyer, K. (1978, December 28). Deranged Workers Pose Problem for the System. *Washington Post*, C1, C13.

Seiden, R. (1966). Campus Tragedy: A Study of Student Suicide. *Journal of Abnormal Psychology, 71*, 389-399.

Seiden, R. (1971, May). The Problem of Suicide on College Campuses. *The Journal of School Health*, 243-248.

Scharfstein, S. (1983, September 6). Why Not Sue a Psychiatrist? *Washington Post*, A18.

Schneidman, E., & Mandelkorn, P. (1970). In E. Schneidman (Ed.), *Psychology of Suicide.* New York: Science House.

Simon, W. (1978). The Ideology of Advocacy: Procedural Justice and Professional Ethics. *Wisconsin Law Review, 29*, 29-144.

Singer, M. (1967). Golden Rule. *The Encyclopedia of Philosophy.* New York: Collier.

Solzhenitsyn, A. (1980). Cited in Berman (Ed.), *Solzhenitsyn at Harvard.* Washington, D.C.: Ethics and Public Policy Center.

Steele, B.H., Johnson, H.D., & Rickard, S.T. (1984, July). Managing the Judicial Function in Student Affairs. *Journal of College Student Personnel*, 337-342.

Stensrud, R., & Stensrud, K. (1980). Attitudes Toward Successful Individuals With and Without Histories of Psychiatric Hospitalization. *Psychological Reports, 47*, 495-498.

Stone, A. (1976). The Tarasoff Decisions: Suing Psychotherapists to Safeguard Society. *Harvard Law Review, 90*, 358-378.

Tanner, W.A., & Sewell, J.D. (1979, November). The University Response Team: An Assessment. *Campus Law Enforcement Journal*, 28-31.

Third Branch, (February, 1983). American Psychiatric Association Takes Position on Insanity Defense. Washington, D.C.: Federal Judicial Center.

Timerlin, M. (1970). Diagnostic Bias in Community Mental Health. *Community Mental Health Journal, 6*, 110-117.

Topol, P., & Reznikoff, M. (1982, Fall). Perceived Peer and Family Relationships, Hopelessness and Locus of Control as Factors in Adolescent Suicide Attempts. *Suicide and Life Threatening Behavior*, 141-150.

Torrey, E. (1974). *The Death of Psychiatry*, Radnor, Pa.: Chilton.

Wilson, E. (1978). *On Human Nature.* Cambridge: Harvard University Press.

Wolf, S. (1982, August). Moral Saints. *The Journal of Philosophy*, 419-439.

Wolfe, R., & Colter, S. (1973). Undergraduates Who Attempt Suicide Compared With Normal and Psychiatric Controls, *Omega, 4*, 305-311.

Wright, C. (1969). The Constitution Campus. *Vanderbilt Law Review, 22*, 1020-1087.

Yankelovich, D. (1981). *New Rules.* New York: Random House.

A Program for Staff Development

     Now that you have had an opportunity to review this publication, we believe you will agree that it is an excellent resource for:

- ☐ College and university mental health professionals;
- ☐ Academic administrators, including deans, program directors, and department chairs;
- ☐ Housing administrators, including resident advisors and directors;
- ☐ College and university attorneys;
- ☐ Members of the campus judiciary.

     The monograph contains seven carefully developed case studies which are keyed to the text. We suggest that you use the case studies as starting points for discussion, analysis and criticism in staff training exercises. Such exercises would be most effective if conducted with participation by diverse staff members, including campus lawyers, administrators, mental health professionals, and residence hall employees. The staff would then be better able to work as a team, avoiding much of the confusion and uncertainty which can occur when a crisis involving a student with an apparent mental disorder does arise.

Complete this form and mail today to order your copies!

------------------------------DETACH AND MAIL--------------------------------

Please enter our order, as follows, for:
The Dismissal of Students with Mental Disorders:
Legal Issues, Policy Considerations and Alternative Responses

One to ten copies:

........copies @$9.95. **Payment enclosed, send prepaid!**

........copies @$9.95. *Invoice on shipment, we will pay shipping costs.*

Ten or more copies:

........copies @$9.50, *send prepaid!*

Authorized by:

. . . .

MAIL TO:

_____

_____

_____

_____

BILL TO:

_____

_____

Resources for Legal Information in Secondary and Higher Education

MONOGRAPHS

If you have found the information contained in this monograph to be helpful in your day-to-day operations and as a reference it is quite likely that you may also be interested in other titles included in the *The Higher Education Administration Series* or in our publications that offer quarterly updates on case law related to various fields of education.

Following is a list of titles available from College Administration Publications. Where the titles are not illustrative of the subject covered, a brief description is included. If you wish to order, there is an order blank on the reverse side of this sheet which you may wish to copy rather than tearing out this page.

Other titles in *The Higher Education Administration Series:*

- ☐ Administering College and University Housing:
    A Legal Perspective
- ☐ Faculty Or Staff Dismissal For Cause
    In Institutions Of Higher Education
- ☐ Computers in Education:
    Legal Liabilities and Ethical Issues
    Concerning Their Use and Misuse
- ☐ A Practical Guide to Legal Issues Affecting College Teachers

PERIODICALS

The following publications offer the reader a quarterly report on recent precedent setting higher court decisions covering a wide range of subjects in the area encompassed by the self-descriptive title. In addition, through the accumulated back issues, and in the "College" publications, a casebook, each of these publications are also excellent comprehensive references that can be of great help in day-to-day operations and long range planning:

- ▶ The College Student and the Courts
- ▶ The College Administrator and the Courts
- ▶ The Schools and the Courts
    While primarily written for practicing administrators, superintendents, school boards, teachers and legal counsel in secondary education, this publication is of great value to related schools of education.

Order Blank

Bill to:................................   *Ship to:*........................

....

....

Quantity   *Item & Price*   *Total*

MONOGRAPHS

_____ The Dismissal of Students with Mental Disorders: _____
    1 to 9 copies @ $9.95; 10 or more copies @ $9.50

_____ Administering College and University Housing: _____
    1 to 9 copies @ $9.95; 10 or more copies @ $9.50

_____ A Practical Guide to Legal Issues Affecting
    College Teachers   _____
    1 to 9 copies @ $4.95; 10 to 24 copies @ $3.95;
                25 or more copies @ $3.50

_____ Computers in Education:
    Legal Liabilities and Ethical Issues
    Concerning Their Use and Misuse   _____
    1 to 9 copies @ $9.95; 10 or more copies @ $9.50

_____ Faculty or Staff Dismissal for Cause in
    Institutions of Higher Education   _____
    1 to 9 copies @ $9.95; 10 or more copies @ $9.50

PERIODICALS

_____ The College Student and the Courts
    Includes casebook, all back issues and four
    quarterly updating supplements.............$98.50   _____

_____ The College Administrator and the Courts
    Includes casebook, all back issues and four
    quarterly updating supplements.............$77.50   _____

_____ The Schools and the Courts
    Includes over 600 pages of back issues and four
    updating reports..........................$67.50   _____

                Postage (if payment accompanies
                order we will ship postpaid)   _____

    North Carolina residents add appropriate sales tax   _____

                             Total   _____

Address Orders to:
College Administration Publications, Inc.
Dept. D, P.O. Box 8492, Asheville, NC 28814

☐ Pricing of the above publications was correct on the publication
date of this monograph. If you wish to be advised of current prices
of titles you have ordered before shipment, please check.

☐ For further information regarding any of the above titles please
indicate with check here and in the quantity column of each publication and we will forward current brochures and information.

PHOTOCOPY OR DETACH AND MAIL